This book is for my daughter, Kairi.
Without her this book would not exist.

paniK

**Candid Stories of Life Altering
Experiences Surrounding Pregnancy**

**Compiled by Melissa Ferina
For Help Inspire Others LTD.**

Published by
Lulu.com
Raleigh, N.C.

Cover Photo by Danielle Rocks (Daniellerocksphotography.com)

ISBN 978-0-578-09355-0

Foreword

Never in my life have I read a collection of works quite like this one. It seems long overdue. Stories that previously had no voice, when the storytellers felt unsure, ashamed, or simply alone, can now be heard. They speak to all of our families, and they can heal, support, and inspire others to share the same voices. Each one tells of a different moment, yet shares a basic sameness — the feelings of panic, whether fleeting or lasting — that we've all felt when the unknown presents itself. *PaniK* allows so many to openly share their tales of pregnancy, parenthood, loss, and new beginnings, from which everyone can learn, despite our own experiences. Melissa Ferina has afforded the writers the opportunity to tell their stories in a way that doesn't judge, preach, or stifle. Rather, she allows them to give themselves over to the pages, with every raw emotion exposed, and we find ourselves sharing their incredible journeys.

For myself, as a working mother of two, finding extra time proves difficult, but I eagerly read each story Melissa received. The fear, pain, anger, joy, and hope kept me invested in every piece. What moves me more is that this book is just the beginning of Melissa's mission. It is the start of something bigger — a project into which she pours her heart — one that can give women and men a forum to share and release, while others find strength and support in hearing their own voices echoed. I am inspired by the individuals behind the words and by Melissa's dedication to the project and this collection.

As you read, I hope you see something in each story, the way Melissa has, that inspires you to listen with an open ear, to share your own accounts with an open heart, and to connect to the feelings we all experience in moments like the ones shared here.

Stephanie Pelcher

Contents

Be a part of something bigger.

Submit your story for consideration for the next book. If you have experienced single parenting, abortion, adoption, stillbirth, miscarriage, or any other life altering experience surrounding pregnancy — submit your story to be a part of this ever growing project.

Send your story to:

Help Inspire Others
P.O. Box 66
Bethpage, New York 11714

Or email your story to
Melissa@Helpinspireothers.com

Include your name, address, phone number, and email address on your piece.

For more information
Visit: www.Helpinspireothers.com

This book is **not** pro-life or pro-choice. It is about real life and what we make of it. These stories you are about to read are full of heartache, overcoming, and strength. Read these stories with an open mind and an open heart. This book has given me a newfound appreciation for what I have and what is yet to come.

In order to keep true to the writer's voice, only minor spelling and grammar changes were made to some of the stories collected. Underneath some of the works, you will find a small quote submitted by the author. Some have chosen to include how things have changed since their experience or what this project means to them. For privacy reasons, some names and places have been changed. The opinions expressed by the authors, do not necessarily reflect the opinion of myself, or the affiliates of the Help Inspire Others project. The authors hold all rights to their work.

Preface

In passing, someone I didn't know very well asked me about my "situation." For a few moments, I opened up about what life is like being a single mom at a young age and how it has transformed me into the person I am today. I shared how my baby's father decided not to take part in her life and how I'm still not sure how I feel about that. There are times I feel I am still waiting for that numbness to wear off. I told her about how I felt being alone and pregnant. I told her how all of my days blended into one. I told her about the nights I wished I'd wake up from this nightmare of "aloneness" and of the utter happiness my daughter's smiling face brings me every day.

I shared my story because 'I' needed someone to hear it, or perhaps, in all honesty, I needed to hear myself say it out loud. Telling my story gave me a small release inside and maybe in turn, began a healing process... Afterwards, this sympathetic listener had a new impression of me and the life I lead as a single parent.

From what I've learned in my 27 years, most life decisions are difficult. No one can tell you the outcome, and many of these decisions are definite. Some people have their choices decided for them. Some have regrets. Some wouldn't change a thing. There are a few choices we may not have control over. These are the ones that just tend to happen. They are also the ones we must learn to accept. It doesn't mean we ever get over them. We just accept. This is what brings out a person's true strength. I had a choice; some did not. These are the people who truly amaze me.

A few days after that eye-opening conversation, I overheard a co-worker talking about my story. If I were hearing the story for the first time about someone else, I would describe it as a journey of loneliness, sadness, and courage. "She is meant for something other than this," were the words that resonated through. Hearing my own story in the third person inspired me. It made me feel as though I needed to take action. To do something meaningful for others like me. This is what sparked the idea for this project. I decided that not only would this compilation be for people who would read these amazing stories, but also for those women and men who have been strong enough to release these stories into the world with the hopes to "help inspire others." In doing this, I hope it provides a release for them as well. It is a full circle project.

Everyone has a story. Everyone has a voice. Each one of the amazing stories that follows comes from people around the United States. Men and women. Old and young. They have experienced firsthand some of life's most difficult challenges — abortion, adoption, single parenting, miscarriages, and stillbirths. Some have spent the better part of their lives coping with deep wounds. Others have discovered a depth of joy that before was unimaginable. Many have been to hell and back.

Each story is unique. Not only have I been touched through the journey of collecting these works, but also I have gained important insights about myself and about life. I am hoping that by sharing these stories with you, you might be inspired; reflect on your own life in a new way. Most of all, I trust these stories will prove that the journey doesn't always go the way it's supposed to or how we think it should. But each one of us has a story to tell that can change another perspective, heal a wound or just embrace someone, through words, with compassion and empathy.

The Single Mother

My therapist advised me to wear my two divorces proudly, to imagine they were Congressional Medals of Honor signifying that I know how to get out of unhappy situations. But with my second divorce, I found myself yet again a single mother, this time a single mother of two boys under five with different daddies. Being a single parent has, until recently, felt like having a disfiguring disability, the kind that makes some people quickly look away while others want to come back, circle around for a closer look. Like many single parents, I've struggled with guilt and felt like I failed my kids. After my first divorce, my dad wrote me and said, "I used to think you were a good person and a great mother, but now…I don't know." My parents, celebrating their thirty-eighth wedding anniversary next month, refer to my brother as "Luke and his family." But for me it's "Iris and the boys." In their eyes, in so many people's eyes, my two sons and I don't constitute a family. But my boys are part of the thirty-eight percent of children in America living in single parent homes. I have been discriminated against. A realtor wouldn't rent to me since "there wasn't a dad in the picture." I once overheard someone on the board of a preschool I was considering say, "We don't want to attract any more single moms." And of course, there's been the dating thing. There was a guy who, once he learned that I had kids, never called me back.

I am writing at the park. William, eight, and Robin, five, are playing in the sand beside me with transformers. Robin just announced, "It's morning time." The transformers are waking up and getting ready for school. When I left Robin's dad (my second divorce) Robin, who was two at the time, regressed with potty training. He started lisping, and he had nightmares. But it passed. Last week his preschool teacher showed me his most recent drawings. He had drawn himself, William, and me, and we're smiling broadly. William's in the third grade; his teacher said he's one of the nicest kids she's ever taught, in her words "a friend to everyone."

We need new words to describe single parent families. Most of the literature about single parent households discusses increased rate of teenage pregnancy in girls raised in broken homes, the higher incarceration rate and the high school dropout rate for boys in broken homes. Are my beautiful boys playing in the sand beside me broken? Because their fathers don't live with us, they're jailbait? I don't accept these pronouncements.

My boys and I wake up around 6:30 am weekday mornings. I make cinnamon rolls or pancakes if there's time before school. We walk up the hill to William's elementary school and next to Robin's preschool, and then I go to class. They think it's funny that I go to school, too. I graduate next year with a PhD in English. It hasn't always been easy. One semester I missed almost a month of school when the boys had chicken pox. Another semester I had pneumonia, but those hard times seem to fade in the overall rhythm of our life.

We are a family. We cook out and go camping. We've vacationed in Florida and California. We go on family bike rides and to the movies. We celebrate holidays and birthdays. We make up some of our own holidays like "Kitty Appreciation Day." We bake cookies together and read aloud. At the end of the day, I snuggle with them, and they sleep soundly and securely. We are a family.

Iris Shepard
Arizona

Lovingly Placed

I no longer remember a time when the word 'adoption' was not synonymous with 'love'. I am a mom for 21 years now, a mom of two beautiful sons — thanks to the miracle of adoption. I tell people my boys are double miracles — the miracle of birth and the miracle of the road that led them to me; adoption. To say it was an easy road would not really be truthful — it was a labor of love — very similar to the labor of childbirth. There is a saying that some of God's greatest gifts are unanswered prayers. I think of that when I think of the road to my boys — one woman praying she did not miss her period, another woman praying she did. That is how it starts you know…and then the two women find inside themselves the strength for the next steps…find each other…and lives are forever changed.

I was never stuck on the idea I needed to be pregnant or be biologically connected to children to love them, to parent them. It surprised me however, that not everyone thought this way. I learned that pretty quickly when I took my sons home and so proudly shared their stories. Some of my friends had also experienced the miracle of adoption and because of what people say, they became hesitant to share their children's stories. However, it only made me more determined — it was my way to advocate for adoption and let others know that families formed through adoption are real families, with real parents and real love. Words surrounding adoption can have negative connotations. People say the birth mother 'gave up' her baby when the truth is she lovingly placed the baby in another's arms. They say 'real' parents when they mean biological (if you pinch me you will see I am 'real'). How about 'are adopted' instead of 'were adopted'? The adoption occurred once; it does not describe them as a person (like you are blue-eyed). Worse is the news media — with the stories of mass murders who, by the way, were adopted.

My sons have known they were adopted from a young age — it was a word we introduced like any other word. Most naturally, they did not understand every aspect of adoption and as they aged and matured, they began to ask very specific questions. Each stage of their lives they've reacted differently to their stories. Very young they thought their birth mothers were rich movie stars; during their teenage years, when they realized sex was involved, they wondered what 'type' of girl she was; as they aged out of teenage years, they began to better understand the circumstances of their birth parents and what led them to me. All along the way, I spoke of their birth mothers as strong women who made tough decisions — and did it all for them. I admire these women — and I am so thankful for them — so my boys came to admire them, too.

My older boy, the concrete thinker — the math major — says he is a combination of us both and is confident in the person he has become. At this time, he says he has no wish to find his birth mother. (This I think will change over his lifetime).

My younger boy, the abstract thinker — the art major — says he would like to meet his birth parents to see whom he looks like and ask those questions. When he graduates college, we will together begin his search.

The adoptions were closed, at the request of the birth parents, but I know I will be able to lead him back down that road. I regret that I did not get pictures of their birth parents to give my boys. Adoption was a new experience for me, so I did the best I could to get through the maze of paperwork, etc. never realizing that one day my young adult son would ask me for pictures. I know these women who gave birth to my boys must think of them. I wish they knew they are doing well and are happy. I will not foolishly tell you that raising two boys was easy because adoption makes it 'different'. Absolutely not! Two year olds and teenagers — tough stuff for any mom! What I will tell you is this: not a day goes by that I don't feel blessed and so fortunate that I had the opportunity to become their mom. They have changed my life in ways unimaginable — I am not just a mom because of them — I am a better woman because of them. They did way more for me than I did for them. Thank you to all those women who make the tough decision to gently place their children in the waiting arms of another woman.

"We all have friends and family who help us through our tough times. But sometimes, as comforting as they can be, they just do not understand — how could they? They have not experienced your situation, have not survived the challenge, the road, you now face. You need to hear that it will be okay one day — okay does not mean it will be easy — but that you will get through this — and learn and grow from this. Other websites may share information on resources and have blogs to share stories, but so many are sharing their suffering. Those of us going through a challenging time in our life need to hear about that light at the end of the tunnel — need to hear that others felt as we do but now are 'okay'— need to hear of successful journeys down this road. We need to hear inspiring stories. Melissa knew that — and understood how just one story could help just one woman face the next day. 'Help Inspire Others' is a gift to us all."

Lisa, 52
New York

Adieu, Mon Petit Souvenir

Dear Bebe,

Once upon a time, I spent the summer in Paris. Most tourists bring home a t-shirt or a beret, but I brought you home.

My little souvenir. All babies are special, but it seemed like you, conceived in the City of Light, were destined to be the most special baby in the world.

I promised tiny ears too small to hear that after we were done traipsing all over Paris and existing on bread and cheese you and I would go home sit on the couch and do nothing but grow.

But it was not meant to be.

Summer ended and Fall started with the doctor's office. My heart fell when I saw that yours didn't have a beat anymore.

I had been thinking for weeks about all the things I was most looking forward to doing with you and because of you - looking at everything with a new perspective. Having you was like having hope grow inside of me. Hope taller than the Eiffel Tower. These are some of the memories and things I will miss -

how we were going to tell people you were coming

telling your Daddy at the Cathedral about you

taking you to the zoo

holding you and feeding you and bathing you
and snuggling with you

your Grandpa bringing you donuts every Saturday morning

Dragging you along on all the crazy trips we take - I was especially looking forward to dressing you in your Paris onesie and telling you how I had already taken you all over the world. Having you with me in those places made it even that much more special to me.

Having you without feeling the need to buy a bunch of baby gear - I knew you were going to be a beautiful, simple creature, coming into the world with nothing and needing little more than love.

taking you trick-or-treating

taking you to the park

giving your dad a son to carry on the family name

Every time I opened my jewelry box and saw your picture there I'd say "hi baby!" and how I thought it was kind of silly - like you were in my jewelry box and not inside me. You were and are inside my heart.

smelling the baby blankets I had found and washed and thinking about how I would wrap you in them and how good you were going to smell

the feeling of you growing inside of me

I was so happy. I was so excited that your Daddy and I were getting to do this together.

I'm very sad now that you are going to leave me, but I'll be ok. I'm going to love you every second you get to stay inside of me until I have to let you go out into the Universe of my fantastical imagination where I have to believe that little angel babies go to play with other little angel babies. I'm not going to believe that the God who let you be created was a mean God when he took you from me. This was just what was supposed to happen.

And after I have to let you go from my body, I will never ever let you go from my heart.

Goodbye, my sweet little baby. I will never get to touch you and hug you and hold you and love you like I get to do with my other "babies" - my love for you will have to be different, but it will always be present. We'll always have Paris.

Love,
Mommy

> "Miscarriage is a common thing happening to many women — but it is also devastating. In this day and age it is hard to believe there are some things left people don't talk about. Miscarriage is all too often a silent loss. Thanks to Help Inspire Others for bringing this out into the open."

Robyn Renee Riley, 39
Oklahoma

Catachresis

I'm pregnant, almost two months
she beams joyfully
tears streaming down her cheeks.

This moment we share again
as in these past three years
each loss worse than the last.

Hugging her sobbing, laughing body
I want to say something.   *I love you.*
She waits for me to say more.

> "My daughter has two daughters
> Their names begin with "A"
> Alexis and Aundrea
> My son has two sons
> Their names begin with "B"
> Brady and Beckett"

Carl Palmer, 60+
Washington

ABBY

The worst day of my life started in the dentist chair, and not for the obvious reasons, although I loathe the dentist. After enduring hours of a tooth extraction and implant screws, I staggered out of the office in a Novocain haze.

Sitting in the boiling hot car, I began to listen to the home messages from my cell phone. Before I could even get to those, many beeps appeared that showed me I had cell messages. Everyone knows I barely use the thing, leave it in my car for days and forget its existence. So with the beeps suggesting many messages, my heart began to pound.

As I listened to one after another, from my son, my ex-husband, my daughter's best friend, and finally from my hysterical daughter, I realized there must be a huge crisis. Nobody told me the extent of the problem, so I drove home blinded by fear. When I got home, there were more messages; call, call, call.

I finally reached my daughter's best friend and she told me the news. The baby my daughter was carrying was dead.

I was beside myself with fear, tears pouring down my face. Finally I reached my daughter; she was in shock and could barely tell me the story. We had talked only the night before, she laughingly complaining that little Abby was quite the kicker. I was so excited to have a granddaughter and laughed with her.

How could this be happening? She was so healthy, everything had been fine; we were planning the baby shower and now this.

She had gone to her regular 8 month appointment, and in doing the ultrasound, they had not found a heartbeat. The doctor had her go straight to the hospital.

As we talked, I kept saying "maybe it's ok, maybe she's fine, don't give up hope". I told her I'd throw some things in a bag and get on the road. In a total frenzy, I tore through the house, clothes, vitamins, shoes all went into bags. I had no idea what I was packing. "Food", I thought. "I need some food for the ride" as I threw leftover meatloaf in a baggie.

I called my husband in hysterical tears and told him I was leaving, told him what had happened. He, too, was in shock and only said, "Drive carefully".

I had no intention of driving carefully. My only goal was to get to San Jose as fast as possible. I defied any policeman to stop me and vowed I would tell him my story and plead leniency.

I knew the road so well, had my "pit stops" along the way and they were markers of progress. King City was the halfway point, a horrible town good only for coffee and bathroom breaks. Passing through this time without a stop, I only marveled that I'd arrived so fast.

I kept in touch with my daughter and son-in-law along the way. She would have to go through labor and they were giving her pitocin to move things along. I thought this was the epitome of cruelty. She would have to deliver a dead baby.

I had been there when my grandson was born and felt the joy in the room and the happiness we all felt listening to the cry of the newborn signaling new life. There would be none of that joy this time, nothing of that sense of accomplishment, nothing to bring home. I couldn't believe this was happening; it wasn't fair, they had done nothing to deserve this pain.

Getting to San Jose in record time, I got lost trying to find the hospital. It was like a bad dream full of wrong turns, dead end streets and strange, scary neighborhoods. Finally I arrived, parked the car and literally ran frantically into the hospital. Finding the labor and delivery area, I was greeted by my ex-husband, his eyes so full of sadness, our shared connection, our baby was suffering.

When I entered the labor room, I found my daughter and son-in-law in tears and mine were joined with theirs. She kept saying, "Why?" and all I could answer was, "I don't know, honey".

They had been put in a labor room away from the other laboring mothers and there was a quiet, very respectful and solemn air about the room. The nurses moved quietly and reverently around the bed and touched her with loving kindness.

All women are courageous when they give birth, but what was being asked of my daughter almost defied description. I have never been prouder of her or sadder for her as she valiantly pushed that baby out. We did not look; we could not bear to see the cord that had apparently wrapped itself around Abby's neck more than 5 times. The nurses took her away, saying they'd clean her up and bring her back to them so they could hold her and say goodbye.

I don't think I have ever felt such sorrow, or had such a sense of impotence because there was nothing I could do to take away the pain. They were so brave, these kids of mine, and seemed so innocent and young. I wanted to hold them in my mother arms and make it all stop hurting.

At their home, knowing none of this, was 2 ½ year old Henry. Thank God for Henry. He was life. He was proof that good things do happen. And he was the reason to keep going. Bringing Linda home from the hospital was made slightly easier because of him. They enveloped him in hugs and kisses, needing to touch him and be reassured that he was real, alive and healthy.

The next few days were filled with family arriving, flowers arriving, and to add insult to injury, milk arriving. I would help my daughter bind her breasts, put cold packages of peas on them to stop the pain and hold her as she wept.

From time to time there was an air of gaiety around the house, almost as if we were gathered for a more joyous family gathering. People brought food and that added to the festive quality. Plans were made for a simple ceremony to honor Abby.

My ex-brother in law is a rabbi and he spent hours with my daughter and her husband talking about death, about grieving and about allowing themselves to feel the loss.

We gathered in the afternoon in their garden. Her brother, father and me constituting the immediate family, and her in-laws, sister-in-laws, aunts, cousins and close friends joined us. I looked around the circle and realized this was the same group that had celebrated Henry's birth.

I stood arm in arm with my ex-husband, all memories or rancor or anger swept away by the love we shared for our daughter. There was a healing of sorts in that moment.

We planted a tree in her honor; we recited poetry, said prayers and surrounded Linda and Tom with our love.

I was remembering all this recently after a visit to their house. The tree is thriving, they are thriving and it warmed my heart. A year ago they were blessed by Sam's arrival. He is a funny, sweet baby and while there is no way to take the place of the child they lost, somehow in his little body, he not only exemplifies love, he has been a healing balm that soothes the wound.

Kathy, 66
California

Coincidence

Anna and I sat in the pale blue and white waiting room, with tile floors so cold our feet felt numb. The walls were filled with posters of young children of every race. Safety tips and guidelines were hung with scotch tape, peeling off from the windows. Brochures overflowed the wicker baskets that sat on end tables at the side of each row. I was reading a sentence over and over from *Parents* magazine, when I realized the room was quite talkative for a lobby. Pairs of two or three women spread out in the waiting room, patiently waiting for their names to be called. Every other woman was filling out a stack of stiff, white papers on a brown wooden clipboard.

"How is everyone so relaxed and smiling?" I thought to myself. I know I would be a nervous wreck. "I definitely know I am, Jessica," she said to me with guilt. I knew for sure she wasn't. "Anna, it was your first time, you couldn't be…impossible," I said without thinking. Her porcelain skin began to flush. I sat back and thought about what I had just said. "Impossible"? How could I think that? I mean it *could* happen I guess. No, this could never happen to her or me. We're seniors in high school, we're only seventeen. "I can't believe *I'm* here," she reiterated to me over and over again. Her signature scent, "Moonlight Path" from Bath&Body Works, began to fade as the sweat built up under her skin. "Listen to me, don't worry. Everything is going to be fine. I know you're not. I'll even take a test too just to make you feel better, ok?" I felt I had lifted some weight from her shoulders.

"Anna," the nurse said, annoyed, "the doctor will see you now." She arose instantly and headed toward the pistachio colored doors in front of us. She didn't even look back at me, which she would've normally done, especially in a scenario like this. Ten minutes passed by, which seemed like an hour, and the same blond haired, chubby nurse pushed through the green colored doors. "Jessica," the nurse shouted louder this time, "the doctor will see you now." I arose slowly and strutted my way toward that nurse with not a worry in mind. I probably laughed and rolled my eyes. Why would I be worried? I was there to support Anna.

"Here, take this and make a right at the end of the hall," another uninterested nurse said to me. She sounded like she'd been smoking cigarettes for years. I held a small, clear, plastic cup with a white cover down the hall and into the bathroom. As I entered the bathroom, I thought to myself, "How am I going to do this?" I never urinated in a cup. I've never even been to the gynecologist.

At that moment, I began to think what if I were pregnant. Nothing dramatic has ever happened to me before. I am seventeen and a senior in high school. I have two married parents, who spoil me rotten, and two educated, successful, loving brothers. I live in South Setauket on Long Island in a big, beautiful white house that I have lived in my whole life. My life has been perfect so far, too perfect maybe. Is God telling me something? Maybe I shouldn't take things for granted. Also, I haven't had that much experience with Tony. Tony and I have been together for six months. He is the most caring, affectionate boy I have ever been with. He's the only boy I've ever been with. He is someone I could never see myself with, but I just went for it. I saw something special, something real in Tony for a seventeen-year-old boy. I know if something ever did happen, Tony and I would handle it, and he would be there for me no matter what.

Before I left the bathroom, I opened the small sliding door on the wall and placed my cup. The sliding door quickly slammed shut on its own. I exited, finding myself waiting in a more private waiting area. "Jess, over here," Anna tried to whisper. I got up and took a seat next to her on the worn blue leather chair. "Did you have to pee in that cup?" she asked me nervously. "Yes Anna, relax," I said to her rolling my eyes like I always do. We waited without saying another word for about ten more minutes and then two women in long, white lab coats approached us. We split up into two separate rooms.

The doctor introduced herself to me politely, and asked me a few basic questions. "How are you today Jessica?" Just by the calming tone of her voice I knew everything was going to be okay. "I'm great actually. I came to support my friend Anna." I said confidently. "Oh?" the doctor looked puzzled. "According to your results, the test has confirmed that it's positive. You're pregnant." The tone in her voice suddenly fell flat, like she was reading from a script. She didn't even pick her head up once from my file. The feeling of surrealism quickly surrounded me. "Now there are four options that can help you make the best decision for you and your child." My blood rushed through my body, and warm, salty tears filled up my big brown eyes, turning them hazel. I stared at the doctor watching her mouth move in slow motion. All I could think about was what will my parents think? How will Tony feel about this? What will the kids at school think? I was here to support Anna, not walk out pregnant. She handed me a Kleenex, like she's done this a million times. She handed me my file, opened the door and directed me toward the desk to pay my bill. As I walked out of the office, Anna walked out too. We didn't notice each other at first because our heads were down with shame. Anna also had a Kleenex in her hand. "I am too", I mouthed to her at the front desk with a clogged nose and puffy, red eyes. "Cash or credit Miss? Miss. Miss. Cash or credit! Miss!" the frustrated receptionist said without sympathy. I was in a daze, with my head turned staring at Anna searching her wallet for money to pay her bill.

We exited the office, broke from our bill, and headed toward the parking lot to my car. We sat in the parking lot for some time as I puffed on Parliament Light cigarettes. "I can't believe this happened to *us*," Anna said with a damp, wet face. "I don't want this to sound mean, but I feel a lot better that it happened to you too. I don't feel as bad about it," she said, part laughing.

Crying became laughing and we began laughing hysterically. We weren't laughing because we thought it was cute, we were laughing because it was so absurd that two best friends were pregnant for the first time together. This is how I handled difficult situations. Anna's first time having sex and she got pregnant! This was outrageous. This is like every older woman's dream, being pregnant with your best friend. We both had a long serious talk about what was best for each of us. We promised not to judge each other's decisions. We swore we wouldn't tell anyone what had happened that afternoon.

I dropped Anna off at home and headed to our high school. I walked toward the glistening and perfectly manicured green grass on the soccer field. I saw Tony from a distance playing a scrimmage with his teammates. I stopped to sit on the muddy metal bleachers to watch him play. I was the only one watching. Ironically, I felt alone emotionally. I knew he would take the news well because he cares a lot about me. Tony spotted me watching him from the field and knew something was up. He took himself out of the game to come talk to me. I told him exactly what I had heard only a couple of hours ago. At first he didn't believe what he was hearing, but then immediately felt sympathetic and wrapped his arms around me. I didn't even feel sympathetic with myself. I think I was still in shock, it all happened so fast and unexpectedly.

Two weeks after that day would forever change our lives. Anna and I chose not to have children and enjoy the rest of our teenage years. We enjoyed being seniors, and went on to college the following year. I don't regret the choice that I made for myself. I chose what was best for me at that particular time. The choice that I made brought me extraordinary opportunities and experiences that I never would have had. I never shared what had happened on that day until now.

Anonymous, 25
New York

Single and Pregnant!
(Yes, with an Exclamation Point at the End, Darn it.)

Well now, how do I start this? Let's see; at two and a half months pregnant, I had to break up with my fiancé. He and I have known each other for 20 years (as friends, then lovers, then friends, then . . . well, you get the picture), and after 19 years of waiting for our "someday", we got together last year thinking, "Finally, our someday has arrived!"

Uhm, not exactly.

We had always loved each other very much as friends, but we were so wildly incompatible as a couple that we almost killed ourselves (and each other) trying to make it work, so we ended up having to go our separate ways. I knew I was pregnant, but I also knew that if he stayed, we weren't doing anybody any good, much less the baby, especially since it got pretty bad there at the end. Was it difficult ending a relationship with someone you had loved for so long? Uhm, yeah. Was I furious, unstable, and hormonally homicidal? Yup. Absolutely. I'll be 7 months pregnant this coming week however, and all in all, I am doing phenomenally well. Quite surprisingly so. I still get geysers of anger (he gets to be single-man-about-town, and I'm home alone — gestating), flashes of shame (I can't believe I'm pregnant and single . . . how humiliating. I'm 34 years old, shouldn't I be MARRIED by now first, and *then* having the kid?), and pouting fits of self-pity at having to go it alone through one of the most difficult things a woman could ever do.

The thing is, these internal roller coaster rides come much fewer and further in between. Somewhere within, I decided that in order to live this life of mine in a way that made any kind of sense to me, I had to lead an *authentic* life. I could not be what someone else expected a woman or a wife to be. I could not fit my square peg into his round hole. I tried, believe me. It almost killed me. I was dying. I came so undone that I got to a place as close to emotional death as is humanly possible and stayed there for 3 whole days — while pregnant. I will never come undone like that again. Not like that. And to be fair to him, he also could not be what I expect in a man; he has his own path to follow, one that could not be deterred by my musings on manhood. He needs to be who he is, and it's probably just not good enough for me. So I wrapped myself up in what little strength I had left and ended it. He made it quite easy, actually. Don't misunderstand me; he is not a malicious person. I cannot vilify him. It's just that he and I will never be what the other needs in this life.

I've had a few significant relationships before, and I was hoping that this was going to be "the one." But you know what? Maybe, just maybe, I am one of those people for whom "Til death do us part" doesn't work. Maybe I can only be at my happiest in this life when I take relationships in doses. Maybe I need to be alone in life, *just as much as I need to be in a committed relationship.* I'm not sure what that will mean for my life, and if my little one will grow up seeing Mom as eccentric because of it, or just accept me as I am. I do know that my kid will be exactly who he is meant to be, who he came to this earth to be, and whether that means falling in love once and staying with that person for the rest of his life, or evolving in this life through the lessons of many gifts of love over time, we shall see. But when I look at the trajectory of my life, when I feel the ineffable blessing that is my little one swimming around inside of me, I gather strength in my ability to live this life on my own terms, no matter how scary and painful that can be sometimes, and I relish in the hope that has returned, the belief that this adventure of mine promises to hold more joy than I could ever know, and the reality that this little boy within me will have a Mommy he can be proud of.

> "The thought of being able to inspire someone to see their own strength within (with my story), makes me feel connected with others. Sometimes our greatest challenges can become our biggest blessings."

Issa M. Mas, 35
New York

If Not I Will Tell you it is Nathan's 2nd Birthday!

Happy Birthday Nathan!!!

Well when I set out to write this I was going to say how much I miss him... and how sometimes I feel sad, mad, angry, pissed, hurt, jealous, and disappointed. But today, well as right now...I feel HAPPY...PROUD...

Two years and nine months ago...I found out I was pregnant. I was scared, angry, disappointed and a little happy... but as time went by, I realized that there was no way I was going to be able to take care of this little baby that was growing inside of me, so I decided to give him up for adoption, to my cousin Sandra and her husband. It didn't work out the way I wanted it to because she found out she was pregnant herself. Sandra introduced me to some of the most wonderful people in the world — Michelle and Greg. From the first time I met them, I never thought that I was making a mistake...they were very caring and understanding about what I was going to do...they supported me and helped me through the pregnancy. I felt this little baby inside of me, I felt him grow, move, kick, and every time I had to go to the hospital or to a doctor's appointment for him, it just got harder, but I had to keep it in my head that I could not keep him and hurt him in any way possible.

On November 15, 2005, I gave birth to a beautiful, healthy little boy. I had a c-section and Michelle and Greg were there...Michelle was one of the first people to hold him...and I will never forget her face when I looked up and saw Nathan in Michelle's arms, the look in her eyes. The love that she already had for that little boy was priceless. I knew right then that I made the right decision. When I was in the hospital, I was alone a lot of the time, I had a really hard time, and I tried to pull myself away from him. The nurses that were there to help my son and me were not helping me... They would bring him into the room while I was asleep and leave him there...so when he would cry I had no choice but to take care of him...because I knew I would not be there for him much longer physically. When I got out of the hospital,

Michelle and Greg brought this little angel to my mom's house so I could say "good bye." I can honestly say I have been through and done a lot in my life but this was the hardest thing. I can't tell you how much or how long I cried because of all of this…and I will more than likely keep crying about him…but between now and then I have been able to see and watch him grow. He has grown into a handsome very much loved little man…he has everything and then some because I love him so much so instead of being sad and upset all day we are going to celebrate the life that I gave him; and the family that he has and the people he knows as Mom and Dad!!! I love you little man…not a day goes by that I don't think about you and how much I miss you and love you.

So Happy Birthday!

Your birth mom, Andrea

Andrea, 24
Michigan

Miscarriage

Lost souls float, belly up, on rivers
as red as a newborn's screaming face.

And I never knew I wanted to be a mother
until the red river ran between my legs.

A river of rejection, of thick mucus, of chunks,
of a stench that creates a fog of mortality.

My thighs were an embankment and
the bathroom floor was a delta.

Splotches of red crashed in waves, permeated
the skin, that carried the message of eviction.

The red river was overflowing and I could not
place enough pressure to stop the wound.

I cradled my stomach as my throbbing throat
coughed out a once living expectation.

My uterus is now an abandoned work mill,
a deserted playground, a condemned beach,
an empty room in an empty house.

> "First, I would like to mention that this poem is written in
> honor of a close friend and her husband. Unfortunately,
> through their loss, I was able to first hand witness the intimacy
> and privacy of miscarriage. It hits our family hard like it does
> for all families involved. This poem was meant to depict a raw
> scene that will hopefully shed more attention on the emotional
> frailty of dealing with miscarriage. I am studying English
> literature/rhetoric and composition at the master level at
> Appalachian State University. "

Victoria Lozano, 24
North Carolina

Dreaming as the Summers Die

I figured something special might be happening that July morning in 1948 when Mama appeared in the bedroom doorway, brandishing her boar-bristled hairbrush in one hand, my not-too-faded red plaid dress in the other.

"Skip the shorts and shirt today," she said, handing me the dress. "Company's coming for lunch."

"Who?" I asked, puzzled. I couldn't think of anybody important enough to wear my Sunday dress for, but I slipped into it, and stood quietly while Mama tugged the brush through my snarls.

I had just turned eleven. No longer in pigtails, I hadn't yet mastered pin curls. So I wore my hair shoulder length and loose around my face, with bangs that forever needed trimming. Maybe I'd learn to set it with bobby pins before I started junior high that fall.

I waited for Mama to answer. "It's Nana," she finally said. "Nana, and maybe Jean." I looked up sharply. Jean was my "real" mother, and I hadn't seen her for years. I glanced across the bedroom at my older sister. Patti and I, just a year apart in age, had been adopted by our "real" father's sister and her husband in 1942, when we were five and six. Patti yawned, and then threw me a wink. Nearly a teen, she was more interested in boys than family gossip.

"Can I go over to Jimmy's?" I asked, as Mama patted my bangs into place.

"O.K. I'll send Patti over to get you when they get here. Just don't get too dirty."

Jimmy lived three doors down and was my best friend. The two of us would climb a towering maple tree to his roof where we would sit for hours, endlessly arguing. I favored the Brooklyn Dodgers and Doris Day. Jimmy loved the Giants and Peggy Lee. I liked Jack Benny, he Fred Allen. Though we rarely agreed, we relished our debates.

A few days earlier we had perched on the roof to watch the July 4th fireworks from the Los Angeles Coliseum. Some evenings we sat up there for hours with Jimmy's telescope, searching for UFOs. We even argued about the merits of the planets. I favored Jupiter, he Mars.

I'd be glad to see Nana, Jean's mother, who always wore sweet gardenia perfume and talked about how she conferred with spirits at her spiritualist church. But I barely remembered Jean. I knew my Daddy Al, of course, Mama's brother, because he visited from time to time. Jean, though, was just a shadowy background figure, referred to in disapproving whispers. She drank, I'd heard. Or she had mental problems, whatever those might be.

She and Daddy Al had married when she was just a teenager, Mama said, and then Patti and I came quickly. Jean just couldn't manage.

More important to me, I knew she was the daughter of a world famous organist, Jesse Crawford, known throughout the 30's as "The Poet of the Organ." Grandpa Crawford sent Christmas cards with photos. I'd heard that he'd had radio shows in Chicago, and was the featured performer at Radio City Music Hall in New York City. My sister had inherited all that musical talent, but none trickled down to me.

"Jean could have been a concert pianist," Mama said once. Jean's brother, Howard, was a musician, too. My taste in music ran more to Vaughn Monroe, than classical. *Ballerina* was my current favorite that year. I'd hum it all the time, but wished I could play it on the upright. Not fair, I used to think. I was the one with the middle name, Jean, so I should be the one with the family talent.

Jimmy and I argued well past noon until Patti eventually appeared. "They're here," she announced, with a smirk and a roll of her eyes. I shinnied down the maple, careful not to tear my red plaid dress.

Jean looked younger than I expected, and prettier, with hair the same dark brown as mine, and freckles, just like mine, sprinkled across her nose. But during lunch she never smiled. Not once. Nana talked of the séances she conducted. Mama talked of how Patti and I soon would be starting junior high. Jean just sat, nibbled at her tuna sandwich, glanced about our tiny kitchen, and looked as bored as Patti.

I wanted to ask if she had seen *Easter Parade*, my new favorite movie. I wanted to ask where she lived, if she traveled, if she liked to play Parcheesi or Tripoley. I wanted to ask if she remembered when I was born. Which did she like to read, *Coronet* or *McCall's*?

But soon everybody was saying goodbye. Jean gave Patti and me each a hesitant hug. "You girls look great," she said, the first words she'd spoken directly to us all afternoon. I wanted to tell her that I liked her freckles, but before I could speak, they were all piling into Nana's Studebaker.

Later that summer, Jimmy's family moved away and I never saw him again. I, nor anybody else in our family, ever saw Jean again either. She just vanished. Nobody ever knew where she had gone. One afternoon a couple of years after that visit, I heard on the radio that my Nana, Olga Crawford, first wife of famed organist Jesse, had died in an apartment fire at the age of 57.

A few years later I sent for my birth certificate, which had been altered when I was adopted, to show Daddy and Mama as my parents. Astonished, I found my middle name was spelled Jeanne, not Jean. Was this how my "real" mother spelled it?

Grandpa Jesse came to my high school graduation and gave me a Smith Corona portable typewriter that I treasured all through college. Throughout the late '50's, I visited him frequently. He hadn't seen her since she was in her early teens and was uncertain about how her name was spelled.

I saw Daddy Al from time to time until he died in 1992. He had been married to Jean for such a brief time and so long ago. He had neither their wedding certificate nor divorce papers, so couldn't help me with the spelling.

Across the decades I think of her. Was she Jean or Jeanne? Did she read Hemingway or Fitzgerald? Would she choose pistachio or burgundy cherry if she were at Curries Ice Cream Parlor? Did she ever marry again or have more children? Did I have half-brothers or –sisters that I didn't know about?

Later, at UCLA, I spent a year interning for Los Angeles County Department of Adoptions while I worked on an MSW degree. I learned about the adoption rules of earlier days, about sealed birth certificates and efforts to protect birth mothers. I also learned why many adult adoptees feel an urge to know, a need for answers.

Even now, in my seventies, I'd like to see my original birth certificate. Every time I sign my name, Theresa J. Elders, I wonder if that "J" really stands for Jean or Jeanne. And I still dream about climbing maple trees…and about my mother's freckles.

> "I'm hoping the project leads other adoptees to feel free from guilt about expressing curiosity about birth parents."

Terri Elders, 74
Washington

Blood Loss

Born six hours ago, already deceased.

Gone like that, taken to heaven.
"Domenick," belonging to God, how appropriate.
I was knocked unconscious, blood loss.
First thing I heard when aware:
"Complications, lack of oxygen, premature delivery."

Tiny baby, just over two pounds.
Miniature fingers, perfect in my mind.
Small casket, custom ordered, name engraved.
Little recollection of the surrounding supporters.
Big funeral, twenty-three car procession.
Huge gaping hole, never the same.

My memories lie in stories retold.
Desperate to hear his first breath.
Oddly wishing I heard his last.
Motionless baby lies in my arms.
Only picture, Mommy and lifeless son.
Six years later, still salted wound.

Kristine, 23
New York

Forever, My Laura

The calendar may show it was twenty years ago, but it just does not feel that way to me. Memories can come flooding back so clearly — when I allow them. Otherwise, I go on my days with my loss locked in my heart. I can talk about it comfortably now — and have been able to do so for many years. I realized long ago — as this project tells us — that sharing my story helped others. It does not ease their pain, lighten their burden or shorten their grief... but does seem to help in some undefined way. My daughter Laura has a death certificate but not a birth certificate — that always amazed me. My daughter was stillborn at 39 weeks gestation after 12 hours of induced labor. No easy task for me, hopefully an easy passage to 'forever' for my Laura.

People do not know how to respond to this when I share my experience, and they certainly did not know how to respond when it occurred. A close friend had also experienced the stillborn loss of a child a few years before me, so there was someone I could lean on as I cried — and I often think of how I must have burdened her, particularly since all my other friends and family thought it best not to 'bring it up' thinking I might get upset. How I wish someone would have 'brought it up'! Not acknowledging my daughters' passing only added to the pain of our loss and thus became our silent suffering. My husband and I of course always remember her 'birth'? day, and until my mom was too sick to remember, she would send me a 'thinking of you card' every year for Laura. That was sweet and greatly appreciated. At the time of our loss mom was unable to talk about this with me, so I realize this action represented such growth and effort, for I had shared with her over the years how hard it was not to have family support during that trying time. I realize in looking back — the reactions of those around me were common responses to stillbirths. And all those not-so-nice remarks well-meaning people say! It just reinforces that your loss, your heartache, could not be understood.

I still put out a stocking for Laura at Christmas — only my sons and husband know it is for her — perhaps others have guessed by now. I donate in Laura's name to a pediatric facility every year on the date that we would have been celebrating her birthday. My experiences have been put to good use — in Laura's memory. I am very assertive both personally and professionally in my role as an RN, in approaching those who have experienced such a loss. I give out my phone number to friends of friends and family so women can call to just talk. I have directed those in need of support to appropriate services and websites for further information. And now — I share my story with you.

Lisa, 52
New York

KIDS

Girl or boy, I hear my voice asking
from a distance universe
but the doctor kindly shakes his head.
Too small to tell, he says, holding his finger
and thumb close together, not even
an inch apart. At home I find a ruler
and see how girl-or-boy would fit
into a teaspoon.

Twenty years later, I sometimes open
the silverware drawer and there,
sitting in a teaspoon, is a tiny person,
legs dangling over the side, not at all like
an angel, but sassier, like Tinkerbell. A she
after all, and looking at me quizzically,
politely inquiring as to what happened.
I smile at her. Ectopic is too big a word
for such small ears. I'm sorry, I say.
What is life like, she wonders. It is
pretty wonderful, I say. I close the drawer
gently. I think she has forgiven me.
But I am never sure.

> "My story has a happy ending; some years after my ectopic
> pregnancy, I adopted a little girl from China, who is the joy of
> my life."

Julie Kimball
Maryland

Re-Creation

From her usual lonely bench, she watches them
play in the park, enjoying their
weekend family recreation.
When hearing them shout "Mom!"
it's always the same…:

Defying gravity,
seated children slip up the slide
into their smiling mother's pulling arms.
In the field beyond, a happy Border Collie leaps
to fling a yellow Frisbee to its handsome master.
Pigeons near her feet
spit seeds onto the shaded pavement
as a summer wind styles
her disheveled hair to combed straightness.
While the wafting aroma from the hotdog vendor
escapes her nose, she glances down
to her wristwatch,
hands speeding in rewind.
Seventy-six seasons pass by in a blur.
Heavy rains rise to clouds.
Old addictions return to crave.
Then everything
slows
as an autumn twilight
retreats from late afternoon.
An odd-sounding honk of a horn
hides for cover under the hood of
a delivery truck racing in reverse as she,
her face hidden,
strides quickly backwards
around the corner of a little-strewn alleyway,
stopping
to ponder
the remnants of a rusty, dented trashcan
where
wrapped in a torn blue blanket,
a bawling newborn bounces up
into her empty out-stretched arms.

W.P. "Liles" Lane, 41

A Life for Kevin

"Dear Grandson,
You were born yesterday. You weighed eight pounds and
three ounces. And I cried when I saw you. You were rosy
pink and wide-eyed. I fell in love with you the moment I
saw you. Someday, when the time is right, your mom and
dad will give this letter to you. It is important that you have
it. Perhaps it will explain why your birth mother decided
adoption was your best chance for life."

I put down the pen, wiped away a tear, and thought back three
and half months earlier. It was New Year's Day and my sixteen-
year-old daughter Nancy (the youngest of my three children) and I
decided to take advantage of one of the biggest sale days of the
year and go shopping. Living in a small community of about ten
thousand, we drove forty miles to the nearest shopping mall. The
day was cold and crisp and we chatted about the holidays and how
much fun we had on Christmas Day. My son Bob and his wife
lived in our community but our other daughter, Sally, lived in
another state and did not get home often. As our children got older,
my husband Ted and I realized that quite possibly it would not be
long before we may not have everyone home for Christmas. Being
a close family we always enjoyed being together, especially on
holidays. With an abundance of food and gifts, this Christmas had
been no different from many others we had spent together.

We were surprised to find a parking space so quickly at the
mall and soon were making our way through the crowds to our
favorite department store. Finding nothing to her liking, Nancy
decided to try another store while I continued looking. I smiled as I
watched her walk off.

A few days shy of seventeen, Nancy was an attractive brunette
with large brown eyes. A talented gymnast, having earned several
first place state awards, Nancy decided a few months earlier to stop
competition and training. She wanted more time to spend on
learning to drive, finding a part-time job, and dating. Practicing
gymnastics several times a week left little time for other things.

"I am writing this letter to you because we may never meet, and I want you to know how very much we all love you. I want you to know it was out of that love your mother decided she was too young and immature to parent you and decided to select adoptive parents for you."

As Nancy walked out the door of the department store and into the mall's main corridor, a strange feeling came over me. Why was I continuing to watch my daughter walk away? What was so different about her walk that compelled me to watch for so long? And then I realized why my eyes had been glued to her. That graceful, youthful walk that had become so familiar to me was now awkward, heavy and swaying. To my shock and horror I realized my daughter was pregnant! I was too numb to continue shopping. Breaking out in a cold sweat I sat down and waited for Nancy to return, searching my mind for answers. Why had I not noticed before now? Why had she not told me? Was our relationship not strong enough for her to confide in me? Waves of confusion swept over me. Did anyone else know? I thought back thirteen years to the day my friend, who was a social worker, called and asked if my husband and I could act as an emergency shelter home to a three-year-old girl whose mother had just died. Being told that the father was unable to care for the child, we agreed without hesitation. This child needed a temporary home, and we had a home! Our son and daughter, who were fifteen and twelve at the time, were excited at the thought of having a toddler visit. Nancy arrived wearing a pair of yellow pajamas, her only outfit. Her hair was matted and her eyes stared at the floor. The social worker explained that Nancy's young mother had died of pneumonia, the other eight children were with relatives, and the father was an alcoholic. Nancy would be placed in a foster home as soon as one was available, in about two days. Little did we know that cold day in January that the two days would last a lifetime, that we would fall in love with this love-starved child, adopt her, and watch as she turned into a lovely, talented, effervescent young woman. The first months with Nancy were not easy ones. She came to us with a broken heart and spirit, and she longed for her mother and siblings. She was malnourished and her head and eyebrows were lice infested. It took all of us to show her that love didn't hurt, that she could have all the food she wanted, and that childhood mistakes weren't followed with harsh punishments. I turned red-faced more than once in public when Nancy loudly used inappropriate language. One memorable time was at home when Nancy and our children were watching cartoons on TV and Nancy giggled loudly and declared, "Look everybody, Elmer Fudd just knocked the hell out of Bugs Bunny!"

"Your mom is barely seventeen. She doesn't know what she wants to do with her life. She still has another year of high school. I do want you to know that she is an accomplished athlete. She is a warm and friendly person. She loves children so much that she volunteers in our church nursery every time they need help. She hasn't dated a lot of boys. She has known your father for several years but only dated him for about five months. He is in his first year at a private college. I understand he is interested in becoming an attorney."

Nancy came back from shopping. She asked if I was finished. I heard myself answer but felt as if I was answering outside my body. It must have been someone else talking. Surely I was dreaming. Please, dear God! I wanted to wake up. I had a good relationship with each daughter. I knew I had always told them they could talk to me about anything. We had frank discussions about life in general, boys and sex. Had I not told each of them that if the time came they felt they were having trouble controlling their emotions with boys that I would go with them to a physician for counseling! I had done a good job raising my kids, hadn't I? I pulled out of the parking lot and began to drive home. Finally, I broke the silence. "Nancy," I asked, "How long have you known you were pregnant?" She was quiet for a minute, then finally spoke. "About three months," she said quietly. Three months! Oh, my God! She had been carrying this secret for three months! Knowing she had a crush on her boyfriend John, I asked if this was John's baby. She replied that it was. She told him about her pregnancy and he thought she would have an abortion. "Why didn't you tell me," I cried? "I didn't want to hurt you and Dad," she replied. Nancy told me she had not seen a physician so we made plans to call her pediatrician the next day. I told her I loved her and would be there for her. We were silent the rest of the way home, neither of us knowing what else to say.

> *"I have been rooming in with your mother and you the past two days. I have fed you and rocked you. I sang to you, recited nursery rhymes, and I have tickled your toes. I shared my religious beliefs with you and I sang: "Jesus Loves Me" to you over and over. I have examined every inch of you. I know your touch, your cry, and your smell. I have studied every feature of your face and looked for anything outstanding about you, just in case we meet again. I want to remember and recognize you.*
>
> *Your Aunt Sally, Uncle Bob and his wife, your great-grandmother, and your granddad (who has become so attached to you already) have all been here and held you. Enough tears of joy and sadness have been shed to give you a complete bath. And yes, your wonderful prospective adoptive parents arrived shortly after your birth. They have been wonderful while we had our time with you. Your mom could not have chosen better parents for you. I have watched your mother cuddle and bond with you. She has kissed you so much that your face is beginning to chap. She has tried to put a lifetime of love into two days. Every minute of the day is spent on your behalf. We are constantly conscious of the clock as it ticks away our precious time with you. Pictures have been taken with each of us holding you. We smile at you with tears running down our cheeks as we try to hide our grief."*

Being a "daddy's little girl," it was difficult for Nancy to tell her dad about her pregnancy. The three of us hugged as we cried. Reassuring Nancy of our love, we told her we would stand by and support her throughout the difficult days ahead. We called John and asked that he and his parents come over and talk with us. He came alone. He was eighteen and said he did not want his parents involved. He never said he loved Nancy, only acknowledged it was his baby and that he would support Nancy emotionally throughout her pregnancy, labor and delivery.

The pediatrician shocked us when he announced he thought Nancy was in her sixth month. How could this be? How could we not have known? Baggy pull-over tops were in style, but how could we be so blind? Thinking about Nancy agonizing over this for so long was almost unbearable. Two days later an obstetrician confirmed a six-month healthy male fetus. Three days later, on a sunny Sunday morning, I stood next to Nancy as we received Holy Communion at our church. I wanted our church family and friends to know that I loved my daughter and I was going to be supporting her through this difficult time. I had a conference with her school's guidance counselor and I spoke with the school's nurse. Both told me they had suspected Nancy was pregnant. Even though the three of us knew each other on a first name basis, neither called to discuss their suspicions with me.

"By the way, grandson, your name is Kevin, after your adoptive father. Your mom thought it would be less confusing if she put the name your adoptive parents wanted on your birth certificate.

Your mom is only seventeen but she seems much older as she pondered what would be best for your life. You see, your granddad and I told your mom we would support her in any way she needed. She could bring you to live with us but she would be primarily responsible for your care and upbringing. We felt that was necessary for both of you. After weeks of much prayer and soul-searching, she decided she was too young and immature to be a parent. She loved you so much that she wanted you to have a better chance in life than she felt she could give.

Your mom had strong feelings about the couple she wanted to parent you, so she refused to let our state's Cabinet for Human Resources have custody of you. And she set out, on her own, to find prospective adoptive parents for you. And she had three criteria: (1) The couple had to be mature Christians, (2) they had to be financially sound and able to give you a good education, and (3) they had to be unable to have biological children. She called an attorney for information about independent adoptions, and thus began her search.

It was ironic that one day shortly after your mom made her decision to look for adoptive parents that I called one of my dearest friends, who lived in another state, to tell her about your mom's pregnancy. I always called her when I needed a shoulder to cry on or good news to share. I told her that your mom had decided to find adoptive parents on her own and what an impossible task I felt that would be. One day, about two months before you were born, your mom got a phone call from one of this friend's daughters. In that conversation she said that she and her husband of six years had recently learned they could not have biological children and that they were hoping to adopt. Learning from her mother of your mother's pregnancy and search for adoptive parents, she was calling to ask if she and her husband could be considered. After many conversations, a thorough investigation, and much prayer, your mom selected this couple to be your parents. God surely heard our prayers and led us to this point.

Phone calls were exchanged each time your mom had a check-up and ultrasound pictures of you sucking your thumb were sent to your prospective parents."

Nancy went into a difficult labor on a cool April morning. Kevin was finally born in the wee hours of the next morning. He had Nancy's large eyes, but looked strikingly like his father. Nancy had a rough postpartum recovery. She had decided in advance to take advantage of the hospital's rooming-in alternative. Her room had a love seat that doubled as a bed and I was invited to room-in also. I accepted, and thus began our attempts to cram a lifetime of love into forty-eight hours.

Each member of our small family came and held Kevin. It must have been especially hard for my son and his wife. They had been married for eleven years and had recently been told their chances of having children of their own were slim. They had talked about adopting Nancy's baby but didn't want to love and raise a child and risk the possibility that Nancy might want to have her baby back. It would affect our entire family. How could we choose sides?

"Nancy, is John coming to see the baby?" I asked. I reminded her that this would be the last night before the adoptive parents took Kevin home. He had called her throughout her pregnancy but our calls and letters to his parents inviting and requesting them to meet with Nancy and us to discuss options went unanswered. John had been called when Nancy went into labor but he never came. "Oh yes! He's coming tonight," Nancy replied. "He'll be here any time now." I didn't think he would come, but I left to get some supper and to give them some time alone with their baby — just in case he did come. When I returned I could tell Nancy had been crying. "What's wrong?" I asked. "John called. He isn't coming." She said. "He made some excuse. He's not coming, Mom," she cried. Up until that point Nancy was sure John would want to see his son.

> *"It's almost time to leave the hospital, honey. The nurses have avoided us all morning. They tell me they have never had a family like us. We not only saw you but we held you, roomed-in and bonded with you. My only response was that it was extremely important to each of us that you felt loved from the very moment you were born. You needed to be rocked, sung to, cuddled, kissed, and caressed by your birth family who love you so very much. We needed this time also.*
>
> *Kevin, it's time to go. Your life is ahead of you. I'll always know where you are and what you become. I'll try to stay out of your life but will always hope and pray the day will come when you will want to meet your birth family. And if you do, your mom and dad know where we are."*

My husband was an emotional wreck. My son and daughter were trying to comfort him in the hospital cafeteria. Not wanting to let Kevin go, he went to Nancy's room and begged her to reconsider. She told him she, alone, made up her mind. She wasn't pressured by anyone and she felt she had made the best decision for her baby. My son took my sobbing husband home.

The plan was for me to take Nancy home and then the adoptive parents would take Kevin home. But at the last minute the hospital balked at that even though they had all the necessary legal papers. They said the birth mother must carry the baby out of the hospital. I took a picture for the adoptive parents as they dressed Kevin in the nursery. Nancy was helped into a wheelchair and Kevin was placed in her arms. Accompanied by a nurse, Nancy with Kevin in her arms, the adoptive parents, and I rode the elevator down in silence. As we went through the hospitals front door, I looked back to see the nurse in tears. I held Kevin as Nancy was helped into my car. She motioned for me to bring Kevin to her. She tenderly took him in her arms and gently kissed his forehead. As long as I live, I will never forget this moment. One single tear fell down her cheek as she handed him back to me. I told her it was not too late to change her mind. She shook her head no and I walked to the adoptive parents and placed Kevin in his new mother's arms. I hugged her and walked back to my car. We drove off, never looking back.

When we arrived home I helped Nancy into the house, checked on my husband, and began unloading my car. The last item I unloaded was the infant car seat the hospital gave to all new mothers. The adoptive parents brought their own car seat so this one remained in my car. I put it in the garage, ran my hands over its empty seat, and for the first time cried until I had no more tears. The strength I felt I had to maintain and display for everyone else finally fell apart. I don't know how long I cried but it was a cry for my daughter, for the birthdays and Christmases I knew would come and go without Kevin being there. I cried for my husband and me, for our empty hearts and arms. This was for our first grandchild, maybe our only one. I cried for the adoptive parents who were beginning an incredible journey, and I cried for the adoptive mom's parents (our long-time friends) who now had what we wanted — our grandson!

Perhaps someday my doorbell will ring. Standing on the other side of that door will be a young man. He'll reach out his arms to me. I'll close my eyes and once again I will recognize that same touch, smell, and love from so long ago.

"Kevin, always remember that your birth mother did not abandon you, and she did not give you up. What she did give you was a chance at life!"
    Love,
Grandmother

Footnote #1

It is now 1997 and Nancy is now twenty-five. She has been married and is presently divorced. Out of that marriage came our granddaughter. She has brought much joy into our lives. Kevin's biological father is married and lives in another state. Kevin and his family also live in another state. His adoptive parents send pictures when we request them. He appears happy, well-adjusted, and is cute as a button. His grandparents continue to be our very good friends; however, we do not have as much contact with them as we once had.

In trying to make some sense out of all of this I came to this conclusion: Looking at the beautiful smiles in the pictures Kevin's parents send us I no longer question what might have been if Nancy had made a different decision. Today I am older and wiser, and I wonder if perhaps God chose Nancy to bear a child for this couple. One thing I know for sure: The greatest gift a mother can give her child is life — and to give that life the best chance she can offer at the time.

Footnote #2

May 19, 2007 — God surely does answer prayers! Today, in response from an invitation from Kevin and his family, Nancy, her daughter and I attended Kevin's high school graduation and party. The night before, we met him and held him in our arms, once again, after eighteen years. He is a handsome, well-mannered, interesting young man. His parents have done an exceptional job of parenting. I hope we will stay in touch. I will respect his privacy if we don't. All our doors are open to each other. And for this I WILL FOREVER BE GRATEFUL AND GIVE THANKS.

"Time really does heal. But it took a long eighteen years for my heart to heal completely. Even though I felt my daughter had made the best decision for her baby, it hurt not to have him in our lives. But the day I had him in my arms once again melted those eighteen years away. We now have a good relationship with Kevin. He knows he has two families who love him, welcome him any time, and take pride in the man he has become."

**Sandra
Kentucky**

When it Rains...

For years I had been imagining what it would be like to be a mother; being pregnant, giving birth, breast feeding and watching my child bloom like a flower, from my womb into the world. I imagined teaching her all the things I know, taking her to places I have been, teaching her about her American and Brazilian heritages. I wanted to relive my childhood memories in Salvador and Rio de Janeiro in her company. Explore with her the smell of the sea, the warmth of the sand, the bright colors of nature in a tropical country, under the bluest skies I have ever seen.

When I found out I was pregnant I was ecstatic! My due date was December 25th...a Christmas baby. My husband and I were planning the design of her room, the colors of the walls, the placement of the furniture and the artwork on the walls. The world around me changed; nothing was more important than welcoming this baby that was evolving inside of me. Every time I looked at myself and my protruding belly in the mirror, I saw a side of me that I had never uncovered — tender, gentle, blissful, and very blessed.

It was a gray rainy day, the day of our second ultrasound visit. I was 18 weeks pregnant and showing. Right away we found out from the ultrasound technician that the baby was a boy! He was yawning, sucking his thumb and moving around in his confined pool. Now that I knew the gender, my dreams become more vivid and reality began to sink in. Our baby boy had a name and an identity. My husband and I were talking about baseball, sailing, camping, and other activities that we thought our son would love to do.

There was a knock on the door of the examination room. The doctor came in with a solemn expression. I felt my heart sink, and I could not breathe. He informed us, as objectively as he could, that the baby had a diaphragmatic hernia. His intestines were filling the chest cavity and they would prevent the lungs and heart from developing. He would survive only while inside me. He would never take his first breathe of air. I could not hear anything else he said. His mouth was moving, but I could not hear sounds. The room turned dark and cold. My mind was racing, trying to make sense of the news. I asked my husband, "what did he just say?," but he was crying and squeezing my hand. As we left the clinic, it was pouring. My face was wet, from tears hidden in the rain.

In the following week, I immersed myself in research and a marathon of appointments. Second, third, and fourth opinions lead to the same diagnosis. In the state where we live, late term abortion is legal up to 20 weeks. After much counseling, soul searching, grieving, and sleepless nights, my husband and I decided to have an abortion.

We chose the most experienced and humane doctor we could find, someone who could hold our hand through the most painful experience we would ever endure. But there is nothing humane about late term abortion. I try to spare myself from thinking about what the procedure entails, so the image can escape my mind. It was over quickly. As soon as I awakened, tears ran uncontrollably and silently down my face. I felt the burden of the void inside of me. His spirit had moved on. I was alone…

When I arrived home, there were flowers, cards and meals on the front porch. Friends and family came by to show their support, but were not sure what to say. There were many awkward moments of silence. I took comfort in the stillness of the air around me. There was no body, there was no funeral. It felt as if my son never existed. I began to write him letters and to remind myself of the butterflies I felt in my stomach each time he swam around. I walked into his room, partially arranged, and touched each piece of clothing. I set all the flowers in his room so he could make himself at home, even if just for a little while.

Today, I still can't make sense of this experience. I have to hold on to the belief that my son chose me as his mother for a purpose. Maybe it was to teach me about courage, compassion, and forgiveness. His arduous journey was brief, but he will be loved unconditionally through the rest of my life. I still talk to him often; I thank him for allowing me to hold him inside my body and soul.

There is a special fountain in my garden surrounded by river rocks; one has his name on it. I plant my favorite flowers there. I look for inner peace and mercy. This special place brings me serenity, but never closure. Though I know his spirit has forgiven me, I have yet to forgive myself for ending his life. On rainy days, I go outside and allow the tears to run down my face and my soul to be cleansed. Drenched by the rain, I picture his face. In my mind's eye, he appears, with the purest smile, while I cry. For a brief moment, I find redemption…

Four years after my abortion, I was blessed with the gift of life again, and this time I delivered a daughter. But my second pregnancy was very difficult. I was too afraid to dream, to plan and to imagine. Each appointment with my doctor gave me a sense of panic. I was not sure if I would ever be a mother again until I embraced my daughter in my arms. She was so beautiful…I felt undeserving of this innocent little being in my arms and guilty that her brother had a heartbreaking fate. With time, I learned that my daughter will not replace my son, and that the wound, still deep from losing him, never ceases to ooze. But most importantly, I have also learned that as mothers, our hearts are immeasurable and capable of loving all the children we bear, in life and in spirit. Finally, I have found true comfort in motherhood. I realize how fortunate I am, in spite of all the pain I have endured. Without my daughter, life would be unthinkable.

Suzy Silva Newsom, 38
North Carolina

Ready

So I sit here in my pink room clawing at the scab on my knee.
I hold my leg up to the wall, the pink on my wall matches the pink
flesh under the scab. I don't like this room.
"Hun, are you gonna help?"
My mom hands me a paintbrush.
"Do you think she'll want to meet me?"
The question remains unanswered, and I sit waiting.
I love my mom…my adoptive mom.
She's the only mom I've ever known.
But deep down I will always feel slightly disconnected.

Ten years gone. I'm eighteen.
I guess I was a mistake to her then and I am a mistake now.
My trouble: I was adopted.
Holes, cracks, jelly donuts,
they all are filled, patched up, enjoyed.
My sense of knowing: empty.
I phone my bio grandparents, they are ecstatic,
say they will call again.
Never call again.
If I didn't feel worthless before, I do now.
I don't resent being adopted. Not at all.
But please, I've been waiting eighteen years to meet her
and she can't even send a picture.
I know she has a two month old son.
No doubt brought back those feelings.
Sixteen and a screw up.
I feel like a hunk of my heart is driftwood, sailing away
the longer and longer she avoids my calls.
I'm rotten that's why I float away so easily.
Maybe if I give her ten more years she'll come around.
Doubtful, she didn't want me then
she doesn't want me now.

Is there something so wrong with
knowing the woman who gave you life?
I am her child.
I have half her genes and I don't know her.
It eats away at me sometimes.

I am happy though, just feel
a tad displaced. It's hard not knowing.
My solution: wait, she'll come when she's ready.

Nicole Christine Banocy, 18
Missouri

Finding Out

It was like a photograph
flaw, a distraction
to the picture I saw,
a floating speck
stuck in a peripheral orbit
on the outer iris ring,
moving out of sight
when I tried to focus on it.
Like a rabbit soon to be caught,
two pink bars appeared
as stained tracks in the snow.
I received confirmation
on the phone with the doctor
while driving distracted through traffic.
I guess I expected a flood
of awareness, a biblical sense
that something had taken place,
that, two by two, cells
multiplied exponentially
from a single chosen pair.
But you came so silently in,
like a ghostwriter
on someone else's life story.

Melissa Guillet

Soft Letters

The word *adopted* with its soft letters,
the p nudged against the t.
Adopted should be a word of nested boxes
instead of the barbed wire
you've erected between us.

It is on your birthday I miss
our never having interwoven.
You inside me
curled against your coming out,
our blood mingled so that what I ate
you ate, what I breathed in, might have
breathed to you there in the sac,
the warm sea of your beginning,

but we were never yoked and that
for you has made all the difference.

First Name

Before she wrapped the blanket,
tucked its ends, handed you
to the agency lady,
what did she call you?

And when, years later,
you tracked her down.
on a tree-lined street
with other daughters
entitled to her arms,
was there a name
that anchored you
to blood and salt?

When you were mine,
I gave you the best I had,
my father's gentle name,
withheld from two sons
for you, my daughter,
a link to my blood
I wish flowed in your veins.

C B Follett
California

In My Innocence

"I hope that when you have a daughter she is as horrible to you as you are to me!"

I shift in my seat on the living room couch and stare blankly at my mother. If I love her I don't feel it. I am thirteen. I stare at her bulging belly; she is pregnant with my soon-to-be sister Ani. I can never remember what had transpired between us that afternoon, why she had said what she did, but I am convinced that hearing her utter those words somehow altered the future. The arguments that would erupt between us in the ten years that followed would be venomous, malevolent, and would leave me completely shaken.

I always make decisions with my gut.

"I'm going to start looking for an apartment," I told my mother one quiet evening after dinner. I was twenty-three. I wanted a life I had tried forcing her to give me — a life that demanded unconditional freedom. She still ransacked my room, opened my mail, and eavesdropped on phone conversations until I had a private phone line installed in my bedroom. Not surprisingly, we fought. She accused me of abandoning her and disrupting the family unit. I moved out and she disowned me for a year, but I knew all along how necessary it was. I had also heard that a mother's love is boundless.

"The embryo is intact," my obgyn tells me.

I spent my 20's trying to recapture a childhood I didn't have; I had slumber parties with my girlfriends, stayed out late until dawn sometimes, I threw parties at my apartment — the thrill of freedom so exhilarating that it felt unreal. Strangely, I felt an innocence that accompanied the newness of my life, and I wasn't willing to give it up until I met Brian. And then I realized I didn't have to give up anything. He loved me and accepted me for who I was; he was warm and passionate, playful and at the same time responsible.

When I married him I shook off the creeping sensation of adulthood by spinning it into my own new reality — I had found a playmate who wanted to share my carousing lifestyle with me. Even when we bought our apartment — an experience that Brian jokingly claimed "drained the adolescence right out" of him — it felt less that I was an adult, and more that we had a secure place to live and have dinner parties.

"I'm worried for you," my mother told me when I was married after four years and not pregnant. "I'm worried that if you don't have a baby you will regret it when it's too late. Think of all your friends with babies and how you two will feel going to baby birthday parties with no baby of your own. It's a sad thing."

To me, a sad thing has always been not doing something out of fear when I know it's what I want. It is why I left my mother's apartment and why I married Brian. I had to stick my fingers in my ears and chant loudly, "LA-LA-LA-LA-LA," to really know that I wanted a baby. Not because my mother wanted one, or because when we went over our friends Randy and Laura's house their son Logan was precocious and alarmingly entertaining. When the decision came whether or not to have a baby, both Brian and I were perplexed.

"We couldn't travel," I told him grimly as I sipped my glass of wine.

"You're not wrong," he said, holding the same serious expression as mine.

"I don't get how people just *do* it!" I said, feeling something akin to anger. "You can do your very best job and they could still turn out to be a crack addict." I realized how cliché my argument seemed, but it was one of many on a long list that truly frightened me……

Magically, I was pregnant after one month of trying. The exhilaration of that felt unreal as well; it had happened too easily.

It was right before my thirty-sixth birthday when my doctor confirmed the news. I had friends coming over that night and had taken the day off from work to cook for my dinner party.

"I'm bringing over a special treat," one of my girlfriends told me, referring to the bottle of Patrón tequila she always brought over for special occasions. I didn't feel right telling her yet, or anyone else for that matter. I wanted a birthday party, not an "Aida's pregnant" party.

"I'm actually on antibiotics for an upper respiratory infection," I told her. "I can't really drink."

Everyone who came that night seemed to believe my lie, and they all crowded into the kitchen with their cigarettes because Brian had stressed to them how the smoke really affected my breathing. But I had a secret and I relished keeping it for the time being. Yes, I was sitting on my couch alone nursing a glass of club soda — but who cared? I already had fantasies of our son or daughter, three or four years old, sitting in bed with Brian on a Sunday morning, both of them engrossed in whatever cartoon they were watching on T.V. I had an image of what our child would look like, taking the best features of both Brian and I and synthesizing them into a little human being. He would have Brian's big brown eyes, his graceful feet, his ability to not take everything seriously; he would have my passion for cooking, my thick brown hair and mischievousness. Admittedly, I wished for a boy. The idea of having a girl scared me. As the years had passed I remembered that afternoon with my mother when I was sitting on the couch, and felt cursed by the inevitability of her wish.

"You're going to have to go get a sonogram. The bleeding could be nothing, but you should double-check." Click.

My mother's care for me seemed inspired by a checklist of responsibilities that she had conjured up — perhaps from her own mother: daily baths, packed lunches, nice clothes, pocket money, and maybe things that I was still unaware of. I knew the two traps that most mothers fell into: they either did the exact opposite of what their mothers had done, or they fatefully turned into what they feared the most — their own mother. I vacillated between this haunting anxiety and an extreme optimism where I reassured myself that I would take what I admired about my mother and practice it accordingly.

"You can still have a life after having a baby," one of my girlfriends told me. "It's what you make of it. Of course you can still have dinner parties and still do your writing. Everything just needs to be modified a little bit." After my thirteen-year emancipation, I was worried that I would resent not having the freedom I had grown accustomed to. And although I was a woman I still didn't feel like one. In my mind, I was a responsible pregnant teenager, who abstained from cigarettes and drinking during her pregnancy because she loved herself and her baby enough to keep both healthy. The reality was that I was in my mid-thirties, happily married, owned an apartment, worked a full-time job and was five weeks pregnant.

"Let me check the book," my cousin Jacqueline told me. She had two young daughters and had miscarried once after they were born. "Would you be having your period right now if you weren't pregnant?"

"No," I said, cradling the phone between my ear and shoulder as I got dressed in the women's locker room at my gym.

"Have you been overdoing the exercising?" she asked.

"No," I said. "I've been very careful. Just walking and lifting low weights."

"Hmmm," she said, and then paused. "What did your gynecologist say?"

"That I have to wait until Monday to get a sonogram."

As I walked on the treadmill I saw an Indian woman sitting across from me, pedaling on a bike energetically, her pregnant belly bulging under her t-shirt. I approached her and asked her how many months along she was.

"Eight!" she said, wiping the sweat off her face with a towel. Hesitantly, I told her I was five weeks pregnant.

"That's great!" she said. "Just keep at it with the gym. Go slow, though. And congratulations!" I suddenly felt renewed. It was just spotting, that's all. I knew it was very common.

By the next morning I knew to call into work to say I wasn't coming in. I made an emergency appointment with another gynecologist, since mine had not been very helpful about seeing me as soon as possible.

My mother called early afternoon. "What did the doctor say?"

"She said the embryo is still there, but that I have to rest."

I laid in bed watching cooking shows, feeling the tugging sensation below my stomach turn into severe cramps. I sat on the toilet, trying to shake the draining feeling that began to overwhelm me. I sat, crying, not wanting to get up because I knew I would only have to return. I called Brian and told him to stay at work.

My mother called again. "What's going on?" She was infamous for her follow-up phone calls — anything ranging from a new recipe I was trying out for dinner to whether or not I had remembered to rsvp for a relative's wedding.

"What's going on is that I'm having a fucking miscarriage!" I screamed into the phone. "And I want you to do me the goddam favor of not calling every half hour so I can tell you about it!" I hung up the phone sobbing.

"Are you happy?" I screamed at the phone. "Now we don't get to find out if she'll be as terrible to me as I was to you. Are you happy?" I knew I was yelling not at the mother I had now, but the other mother I was scared to forgive.

At least I had the weekend to recover. There was no baby. No little boy or girl sitting in bed with Brian. Neither of them would look at me with the same large brown eyes.

A week later Brian and I went to a nearby park where we took our dog Champ for long walks. We sat on a bench that overlooked the lake. Although it was April, we could still see our breath form little clouds in the air. I watched the geese padding around the edge of the grass. I grew quiet.

"Are you okay?" Brian asked. "What are you thinking?"

Now I knew what it felt like to want to hold onto something so desperately that it was consuming. I wondered if that was how my mother felt all those years fighting with me — if it was her way of trying to hold onto me for her own reasons that I could not understand.

"I'm thinking how strange it is. I'm thinking how I feel so changed, that I'm not the same person. I feel," I said, trying to find the words, "that I have lost something. Not a baby only. It may sound terribly foolish coming from a grown woman, but I think that somehow I have lost my innocence." He took my hand and squeezed it.

Prophetically, a little girl came towards us, wobbling on her bicycle. She looked behind her where a young man was standing, most likely her father. "You're doing great!" he called out waving. "Keep going! I'm right behind you. I'm watching." I watched her as she pedaled away, her father following her with his eyes. It all seemed too easy. And I knew then that everything I had so desperately wanted in my life I had struggled for. I am waiting to find out if I am still willing for this struggle.

> "Help Inspire Others has allowed me to share my work in an arena that would otherwise not exist. This experience has helped me understand my limitations when it comes to living in the gray area of life and accepting them. I still struggle with this, and think I always will."

Aida Zilelian, 38
New York

My Pregnant Adoption

We were expecting a baby. Actually, we had been expecting one for nearly seven years. But now as we set about putting together the nursery, it was obvious to us that a baby would come one day soon. Still, no one outside of our family and close friends knew of the upcoming event. So one day I had an idea. I called my cousin Bonnie to see if she thought that my idea was good. She had been pregnant twice so at least she had the experience of knowing what pregnancy was all about.

She thought it was a great idea! So we eagerly set about making plans for my "pregnant adoption." Bonnie sewed. I had the design. And between the two of us we created a garment that I shall affectionately call "my tummy." The garment looks like a sleeveless maternity top. It is fashioned out of white quilted fabric, the kind you use in quilting. Then, cutting it out, we attached another piece of fabric shaped like an oval and this she sewed to the abdomen of the top. We proceeded to fill the oval-shaped pouch with eight pounds of dry navy beans.

There was our first adjustment, eight pounds was too much. Not only did I look overdue but I couldn't wear eight pounds comfortably on my 5'2, 104-pound frame. So, we took out three pounds leaving five pounds in the pouch and sewed up the slit. There it was — my tummy!

I put it on and felt for the first time, the thrill of having a protruding tummy. I definitely looked pregnant and even though, at the moment, I could see that it was a garment, a part of me said, "Baby." Then I slipped my blouse over the constructed top and realized that it would not fit. I made myself a promise that if I had the courage to wear my tummy, I should also have at least one maternity top to complete the picture. My cousin and I made a date. The following week we would have dinner and go maternity shopping. Until then, I had already two to three bulky sweaters in my wardrobe that I could wear.

The first couple of days were exciting and revealing. I wore my tummy at home in private. My husband was understanding and supportive, but I hadn't as yet ventured out in public. I warned him ahead of time that I would. Careful not to offend me or squelch my enthusiasm, he took this in stride.

As I walked though my daily routine I would find myself touching my tummy gently and imagining that I was carrying our baby. At times, the feeling was so real to me that I forgot that it was a garment that I had on and not a part of my body. I was conscious of what I was eating and alert to my fatigue, which was a signal for me to rest. I felt like taking better care of myself and I did.

Then came my first "showing." My neighbor Nina, also an adoptive mom, wanted to drop by to return something, so I invited her in for coffee. But I felt it necessary to forewarn her ahead of time that I would look different. Having told her about my idea to experience a pseudo pregnancy, I merely told her that I was wearing my tummy. She responded too genuinely and casually that I forgot I had my tummy on while she was there. We sipped coffee while her toddler Erik explored the confines of the dining room and stairs. I felt pregnant. It was a spiritual feeling. Something made me aware that there was a life soon to enter ours. I was every bit as expectant as I imagined I could feel.

The next week came and I was going out in public. This meant I was about to expose to the world outside our door the news that a baby was on its way. Fortunately, I had two coats that were voluminous and that there was enough room for my tummy and me that winter. People's reactions to seeing me were curious. As I walked through the shopping center, my cousin, who was walking with me, pointed out that a man had just looked at my tummy. I smiled. "They can tell!" I thought to myself. It was a tiny thrill, and I liked the way it felt. One of the things I had missed the first time as we waited for nearly five years for our now seven-year-old son Ben was having someone acknowledge me. Going in the ladies room, one woman smiled at me as she looked at my tummy. I looked at her obviously pregnant tummy and smiled back. Another woman who had a young child with her smiled and asked, "Is this your first?" "No," I said, "I have a seven-year-old son." When she asked me what I was hoping for with the second one I replied, "A girl." I did not explain that we were assured of having a girl when she replied, "I hope you get one."

There were other times that my creative pregnancy caused responses from others that were surprising and fun. My sister-in-law was about to stop me as I bent over to pick up a fork that had fallen on the floor and do it for me. Then she realized that I needn't exercise caution and we both laughed at the touching scene we created at a family gathering. She forgot that it was a garment that I was wearing and so did I. Others around us had forgotten too as they smiled at the kind symbolic gesture. I was visiting a friend when she asked me how I was feeling. When I replied, "Tired," she said, "Well that's to be expected," completely forgetting for a moment that I was not pregnant tired, but tummy tired.

My sister Paula regaled me with stories of her pregnancy when I was visiting her home in Madison, Wisconsin. I relished every detail as if I had heard it for the first time. Rather than follow in total ignorance of what it must be like being pregnant, I could now listen with some experience. I waddled too. I had to lay on my side when I rested. I had back pains. I had difficulty putting on my shoes. I was inches further from my kitchen counter and had to bend as I cooked. I rested my hands on my tummy and dreamed about the baby.

On more than one occasion, Ben rested his head on my tummy and I was so overcome with the tenderness of that moment. We talked about the baby, perhaps more, because she was so real to all of us especially when I wore my tummy. There was an outward sign of the baby. Even my skeptical husband, patted my tummy.

Adoptive mothers miss out on a lot of the drama-building events of a pregnancy because there is no visible sign of their condition. Worse, the waiting is so long that it can be real painful to be asked, "Have you heard anything yet?" I not only noticed things when I was wearing my tummy, I noticed things when I wasn't. My son and I went to look for a chest of drawers for him because his matched the crib, which would be given to the baby along with a new quilt and bumper pads. The store was filled with pregnant women looking at the many nursery sets that were for sale. These women all had protruding tummies of various sizes. This day, mine happened to be flat. I really felt alone. I was sad that I could not announce too, that I was buying the quilt for the baby we were expecting. It struck me that I had become attached to my tummy and felt different when I was not wearing it.

Oh, there were conveniences to my "removable" tummy. I took it off when I slept, got tired, or jogged. Also, there were places that I felt I could not wear it because I thought people would be confused such as in church. Perhaps if I had more confidence, I might have tried. I also had to be sensitive to my husband's feelings. He was being adaptable. I had to be considerate not to push him to where he might object.

There were still the subtle and not so subtle limitations for me in wearing my tummy. I could not join the prenatal aerobic classes. I was in the advanced stages of pregnancy according to my appearance and it was difficult to find a leotard to fit. But I thought about it. I did on the other hand have my first experience going to a maternity shop and buying some clothes.

There were things that I did not have to go through not having an authentic pregnancy: nausea, gynecological exams, stretch marks, varicose veins and gaining twenty-five to thirty-five pounds of extra weight. I had only gained five pounds and those five pounds I could detach at the end of the day. I was glad that I missed these things. However, there were so many things that I wanted to go through that I did miss out on, such as: breast-feeding, labor, delivery, our birth announcement in the newspaper and swapping stories with other birth mothers. But because I wore my tummy, I was never far from the reality of feeling that there would be a baby coming into our lives.

Would I do it again? In a heartbeat! Would I suggest it to other women who could not experience a natural birth to venture into another realm and experience a pregnant adoption? Absolutely! My adventure into the domain of trying on a pregnancy was invaluable to me. I have some of my greatest memories of waiting for my little girl and I can honestly tell her, "I carried you!" I have my cousin and my tummy to thank for that.

> "Now my children are thirty and twenty-two years old. They have been the joy of my life. Neither have sought their birth parents and both believe that we (my ex-husband and I) are their real parents. They are as flesh of my flesh. They are as loved as birth children and express a lot of love and affection. We dealt with adoption issues as they grew and are well-adjusted adults. If they decide to do a search, we will support them."

Patricia Rose Gilles, 58
Minnesota

Miracles Do Happen

I had my miscarriage almost 10 years ago and the pain lessens every day but the memory and loss never goes away. I still remember the day like it was yesterday. I can still hear the words echo from my doctor's mouth, my cries and the look on my family member's faces. The ceramic broken heart hung on the door said it all. There are broken hearts in this room. I was 18 weeks pregnant with a baby girl and I couldn't carry full term because I have an incompetent cervix. Basically, my cervix cannot hold the weight of a full term baby. There is not a day that goes by that I don't think about what she would have looked like, what my life would be like if she was here, where is she now? I was not myself for a long time and I was depressed most of the time. Between the physical disability and the mental scar I thought I would never get pregnant or have a child after this happened to me. I was wrong. I had Frankie at 25 weeks pregnant after having surgeries, shots, and weeks of bed rest and hospitalization. I had my doctor visit at 20 weeks. My doctor sent me to the hospital with an 80 percent chance that I would deliver overnight and my son wouldn't survive. Well I fought hard and prayed hard. I wasn't giving up hope. The first day turned into the first week and before I knew it I was there for 5 weeks. My son Frankie was born with a weight of 1 pound 6 ounces. The first thing the doctors tell you is to hope for the best but prepare for the worst. And that I did. The first few days I couldn't see Frankie because I was sick after delivery with an infection. It took me a few times to go in the room with him and actually stay there because I was afraid of getting close to him because he was so tiny. The thought of seeing your baby one day and not knowing if you would see him the next is so scary. Every day was a fight for him and every day I was there for him, watching him grow. He went through surgeries, tests, and transfusions without a fuss. This is the second time in my life I have felt so out of control of the life of my child. Frankie pulled through every obstacle and came home 11 weeks later. He is now 7 years old and the most amazing person I know. He skateboards, plays guitar, plays baseball among many other activities. If you know my son you would say, that boy does not sit still. And I say to that, "thank you God for my Miracle." I feel truly blessed to have such a special person in my life.

I remember the loss of my daughter every day and have now made peace with it. I am no longer angry but sadness will always remain a strong feeling. I thought there was no hope for a long time and now today I realize I was wrong. Some of the best things in life happen even after tragic events. You have to just keep your head up and remember "miracles do happen"...

Danielle Albanese, 32
New York

Poem to My Unborn Child

I never got to hold you
I never gave you a kiss
I didn't think it through
It wasn't supposed to be like this
I wonder what you'd look like
I wonder what you'd be
I want you to know you were created in love
Between my first love and me
My mother made me do it
She thought she knew what was best
At the last moment
I failed this test
I could have saved you
I could have run
At the last moment
I agreed to have it done
I went home childless
I couldn't face my love
All these years later
I can't believe that was me
I was young and afraid, can't you see?
I have always been sorry.
I know sorry isn't enough
I've never forgotten you
Even though that was the plan
My mother is gone now and
I never married that man
My baby how I've missed you
I've dreamed of the life we could have had
I sit here in my room and all I feel is sad
I would have loved you
I would have been your biggest fan
I cannot take it back
Please forgive me if you can

"I was born into a large family but I was raised with only one sibling. I met a boy who said he loved me and I got pregnant. I was urged to get an abortion. I have wondered what or who that child might have been. Now, I am the mother of five. I am forty four years old and my youngest just started high school. I am an aspiring writer in my spare time."

Suzette A. Cozad, 44
Maine

She's so Beautiful

I see her, she's so beautiful
She's cute and plump as she smiles that toothless smile
She looks up at me and touches my face with her little pink hand
It's as if she means to say, I love you too Mommy
She giggles as I make a funny face and kiss her on the belly
She's so beautiful

Her hair grows longer and becomes the same color as mine
She loves when I put it in pig tails and add little pink bows
She hugs me when she's scared and tells me not to go
She always smells like cookies mixed with baby shampoo
She warms my heart and makes me laugh every day of my life
She's so beautiful

She grows as fast as a weed and has dimples just like me
She's kind to other children and likes to ride the ponies
Her favorite color is purple, which she paints upon the walls
She laughs and plays with her big brother; they are the best of
friends
She is so, so beautiful

I wake from this dream; I can still see and smell her
I start to shake and tear as those details start to slip
It was a dream, only a dream of my little baby girl
The hands I'll never hold, the hair I'll never smell
Did she have hands when I let them take her?
Had her heart begun to pump and give power to her growth?
Does her soul watch me from above and
wonder why I didn't love her?
Will she forgive me? Will I ever forgive myself?

She was so beautiful
How could I have not seen that until now?

"Help Inspire Others gave me an opportunity to express the feelings and thoughts that I had been hiding from. It helped me to face the raw truth of the experience, explain the pain I feel every day, and finally start the healing process. It is both terrifying and liberating to share my personal thoughts but I did so hoping to discover that I am not alone, and others could discover the same."

Rose, 30
Illinois

When I Was Seventeen

My name is Danny, and when I was 17, something happened to someone and myself. I'm 22 now, but this experience has always weighed heavily on my mind and heart. Her name was Michelle, we had been dating for approximately 5 months when things started to go sour. I decided to break up with her, and I did. She was upset, as was I, but it seemed for the better. A few weeks after the breakup, during a bomb scare at school, she found me on the field. She said she had something really important to tell me so we walked away a little bit from everyone and started talking. She was tearing and having a hard time saying what she was thinking. I, at the time, assumed she was just going to say she wanted to get back together. However, the words that came out of her mouth truly froze me dead in the spot where I sat next to her. She searched my eyes for an answer to a question she hadn't asked. She'd told me she was pregnant. All I could mutter after a prolonged silence was that I needed time. I got up and walked away from her as she began to cry quite hard.

Weeks went by, and I still couldn't find it in myself to truly grasp the reality of the situation. Soon, there came murmurs that I was an asshole who abandoned his girlfriend when she got pregnant. It wasn't true of course, however, in hindsight I cannot blame her for saying so to her friends. When we got in touch again, which was made doubly difficult by that point by the fact that she had assumed I didn't want anything to do with her; we spoke of adoption. Michelle herself was adopted, and we felt it was the best course for the child if it was to come into this world. We wanted to give the child the best life it could have, even if we couldn't provide that.

However, this did not come to be. Six months later, our baby had passed away. It was severely premature and as a result was stillborn. We didn't talk much after the baby passed. I don't think either of us knew what to say or do really. I'm sure it was easier for me at the time. I didn't have to go through the pain of that experience on a personal level. However, the psychological effects of this event still carry with me to this day. I've had more than one scare in my life which turned out to be nothing. Every time I have had one since Michelle, I think of what happened in the past and I get so angry with myself for letting it happen again. I only really want to bring a child onto this earth if I am fully prepared to accept and acknowledge the responsibility and care myself. I'm not there yet. I would love to be, but at this point in my life, I am not prepared to assume that role. If I had to, I would of course, but I wouldn't be the father I aspire to be. At least I don't imagine so, just because of the limitations that I would have. Life is so precious, a gift. My experience with Michelle only highlighted the frailty that life has. I wasn't prepared for a teenage pregnancy, but neither was I for a stillborn.

Daniel, 23
New York

It's a Process

I have tried to do many things over the course of my forty years. Some I have excelled at and others, not so much. Out of all the unsuccessfulness I have endured, the only time I have ever felt like a complete and utter failure was at trying to getting pregnant.

When Andrew and I first were married in 2000, our main focus was our house and making it into a home, a home that could shelter a family. We had spoken about having children and both of us wanted a few. Around our third anniversary, I decided it was time to make our dream a reality. I came off my birth control pills and we tried — for a year — with no positive result. Before I got married, I was always worried about getting pregnant. Now I found myself struggling. After consulting with my OBGYN, he suggested a reproduction specialist. With all the preliminary testing complete, I was scheduled for an IUI. After two weeks, I took a blood test in the office and was told we were, in fact, pregnant. We were elated and told everyone! By the end of the week, I was no longer pregnant.

We were able to try the same procedure the following month. Again we received positive results, but this time chose to keep the news to ourselves for a couple of months. We announced our elation on Christmas Day 2004. Keara Paige arrived late at night on August 23, 2005 by way of a C-section. She was perfect.

Right before Keara's fourth birthday — after four years of never using any form of birth control and trying every month to conceive, we decided to return to our fertility specialist.

Silly of me to assume that on the first or second try we'd be successful again.

From August to November of 2009, I had IUI after IUI, each time increasing the dosage of Clomid — with no positive result. When

I reached the maximum dose — 5 pills for 5 days — my pharmacist actually questioned me with concern. Taking 1 pill for 5 days is enough to see a drastic change in your mood. 5 pills each day is unbearable for you and the people around you.

In December, I stopped. I needed a break. The stress was overwhelming and work was getting really busy. I was disappointed and depressed. Plus, going back and forth to the doctor was very challenging and starting to get annoying. I was miserable.

In February of 2010, it was recommended that I have a hysterosalpingogram (HSG) to check to see if my tubes were draining properly so my eggs can pass through them. My right side, of course, was blocked. I had to have a tubal cannulation. They pass a wire through your tube to try to open it up and remove the blockage. They were actually able to open it up. Good news. Go me.

From March to July of 2010, I continued with the Clomid and IUI's....still nothing.

In August, we started the injections instead of the pills and had our last IUI. Nothing. When September's cycle started off, it was slow but began to pick up with the injections. We were told by the doctors that they wanted us to switch from IUI to IVF. The cycle was great and everyone was excited because I had developed 11 eggs — the most I've ever had over the course of the year. However, with IVF, comes a greater expense. We had exhausted most of our medical coverage during the year. We felt it was worth it to try.

I was scheduled for the retrieval and they were able to harvest 10 out of the 11 eggs. They were supposed to call me the next morning to tell me how many were fertilized and when to have (hopefully) two put back in. Instead the call came from my doctor. She said she had bad news. Now my initial thought when those words came through the phone was that she was going to tell me nothing fertilized, I would have my answer as to why we had not been successful and I would be done. What she told me made me collapse into hysterics. She said that the embryologist accidentally dropped the dish when she was checking to see what fertilized and she was unable to recover any. They were all destroyed. They have no idea if any took. What, may I ask, do you say to that? My doctor said the embryologist felt horrible. I thought at the very least she should be suicidal.

The irony of all this is that I was talking to my friend Melissa a couple days prior to the procedure and was fretting about all the things that could happen — I was talking about human error and everything that could go wrong. And there is was. I put that negative energy out there and got it back, ten fold.

The devastation was beyond words. There was agony too, due to the pain my body had endured, followed up by some good old fashion misery and depression. I was really fun to be around.

They were very accommodating at the specialist though. They refunded me all the money that I laid out in co-pays. They even refunded what they charged out to my health plan for all the medications. They started me up again in October. They paid for everything. It was the very least they could do because of their carelessness. I still consulted a lawyer.

I endured the injections again and had the retrieval again. This time I only had 6 eggs, they were able to get 4 and only 2 took. They put those 2 back in on November 1st, 2010. There was nothing to freeze for another try if need be.

Two weeks later I went in for a pregnancy test and got the call I had been waiting for over a year. It was positive. I was elated. My first sono was good. My second sono was great — I was able to see the heartbeat. My third sono at 7 weeks 4 days — there was no growth, no heartbeat, just devastation again.

The next day, Andrew called me at work to tell me my grandmother had died. I waited all week for the miscarriage to happen. I finally lost the baby the day we buried my grandmother....December 14th. What I experienced and saw in my bathroom is something I wouldn't wish on anyone. It was traumatic. The worst part of this whole thing was we were going to tell Keara on Christmas morning. That her wish was going to come true. That she was going to have a brother or a sister. Nope, it was not a good Christmas for me.

We had to wait a couple of months until my cycle came back on track to try again....the injections, the retrieval, the whole nine yards. We started up again in February 2011. Not fun at all, but I was trying to be positive and think of what we'd be gaining. I had 7 follicles this time. 3 didn't take, 4 fertilized. 1 was on the smaller side the day of the procedure, so they only put 3 in. Two weeks later I had a positive result again....thank God.

By the fourth sonogram however, there was no growth and no heartbeat. I was 8 weeks, 3 days pregnant. I couldn't bear to go through a miscarriage on my own again, so they scheduled a D&C for me 2 days later for the removal. I bled more than I thought. When I asked why so much, I was told mostly likely it was due to them not getting it all. Wonderful.

We had to wait again for my cycle to try again. I began my injections in June.

So here I am...24 months later.....after countless injections.... painful procedures....2 pregnancies and 2 miscarriages in a 6 month time frame....now waiting to take my HCG shot to ovulate and go for my 4th retrieval. I have 8 follicles at the moment, so — as always — I am hopeful.

Am I crazy for putting myself through all of this torture? Probably. Am I stronger than I thought I ever was? Most definitely. Have there been plenty of times in the past 24 months that I wanted to crawl into bed and not come out....ever? Yep. The only thing that gets me through those days is my dearest Keara. She is the most wonderful, joyous, precious thing in my life — and I am beyond blessed to have her. I've put myself through this for her....for the fact that she has asked me, 'why don't we have a baby? When am I going to have a brother or a sister?' For her words and the love we as a family have to give is why I keep trying.

Along with this double life I have led, I have taken the advice of a dear friend of mine and focused my efforts on my Keara girl. This other life of doctors and office visits and stress and craziness I try to keep as separate as possible. She knows I go, she sees Andrew give me my shots, but I don't tell her why. She doesn't need the disappointment too.

When is enough, enough? Who's to say? After one year? After two? When can you say, 'I've done all I can'? When do you stop saying to yourself, 'what if'? I wish I knew, but I feel there is no answer for me right now. I do think, however, it'll come in the form on an epiphany. So here I am, waiting for mine.

In my case though, I don't think it'll ever come. Deep down, I will never stop hoping. If I gave up, it would be like giving up on the potential of someone, of the possibility of a new life. I owe it to myself and my family to keep trying until I physically can't, or until I finally get to the point where I just don't want to put myself through it again. It's a labor of love right now, so I continue for them, for me. And I'm waiting…and I'm still hoping.

> "Getting my story down on paper was cathartic. I honestly and wholeheartedly feel that I was meant to meet and become close friends with the founder of the Help Inspire Others project. She has been a confidant, a sounding board, and at times, helped me be rational. This project…this friend…has helped me heal."

Catherine O'Neill, 39
New York

Seven Sets of Three Pushes — Ten Seconds Per Push

One night - one night before Halloween. You were you and I was me - your hands all over my body-

We were just nameless-faced-people, we barely knew. And you kissed me goodbye like my feelings actually mattered - like I actually mattered.

For those nine months - I felt ashamed...like I was THAT girl without a name - without a memory of who he was. There was no memory because I didn't know him - I didn't know his last name.

He smoked, he snorted...he drank a lot of Jack.
I became nothing but a girl who slept in his bed.

For nine whole months, I was screaming inside.
Are they looking at me?

EVERYONE is looking at me. There I was - alone...doctor appointments alone...nights spent crying alone...I FELT alone. I was alone.

Her little feet kicking through...she never stopped reminding me that she was there.

In a small room in such a large place - out of all the people around me I felt alone - empty - incomplete.

The other half of the DNA wasn't there. He was snorting - smoking - drinking - doing someone else. Panicked? I'm sure. Worried I'd take the little money he had - worried he'd have to finally grow up - worried he'd have to stop doing drugs - worried he might have to face his own fears - worried he'd have the biggest responsibility a person can take on?

Seven sets of three pushes. 10 seconds per push - and here she was. Looking into my eyes like she had known me forever. Looking into her eyes like I'd love her forever.

Her hand in her mouth - the moment he missed that he will never have. Her first breath - the first cry - the first yawn - he will NEVER have.

I do nothing more than what I can do - I give her everything I can give - I'd like to think of him as a passerby-someone who came into my life just to give me the best thing life has to give. Can I hate him...can I REALLY hate him for that?

I can't. I can only thank him for the donation........she really has such beautiful eyes.

Anonymous, 23
New York

The Miscarriage

I fell asleep beside her
she was dreaming of a son and
I woke to trace the movements of the
dream behind her eyes. We are born
first in the heart, here I felt him
taking form and I moved to shape
a place inside
hollow where I used to be.

She fell asleep beside me
we were resting in the yard, the garden
newly planted, rows of peppers, peas and corn
and the book of names left open
cradled snugly on her lap. She was worried
she was showing — "Something solid
from the church, My parents, you know?"
Maybe Matthew, not too mystic,
no, not Peter, maybe John?

When she woke me I was dreaming
in that half world where I live; he was
riding on my shoulders
— all the things I never had —
and I heard her in the bathroom
was she weeping? He'll be tall —
I'd been reading all the doctor books
and learning DNA.

Then I fell asleep beside her
she was dreaming of a son and I
felt her soft and pulsing
supple warming of her skin.
And the hand that stroked my cheek
clenched and hardened into stone,
how I kissed and blessed what fell
asleep in the darkness of her womb.

Ed McManis, 54
California

The News

Friends,

This has been a hellish week.

I detest such form letters. I have never sent one before and I hope to never send one again. But I must. The news. For many of you, those I haven't had the chance to talk to in a while, it will be news that Emily was pregnant. She is no longer. She miscarried early Wednesday morning. She was four months along.

To say that this is hellish for us, or traumatic, makes what we experienced seem really trite. Emily had had a lot of trouble with this pregnancy. Almost every aspect of it was different from her first. Earlier this week, she had what we now know were contractions. She spent Tuesday in a hospital in Richmond, but they sent her home.

Late Tuesday night, her water broke. I was with her when she delivered the baby. There was absolutely nothing we could do. She held him as he died. It took an agonizingly long time.

We named him Abraham Wilson.

Emily spent the remainder of the night in the Farmville hospital. Our neighbor, Claire, was able to come down to the house and stay with Thomas. He did not wake up. The ER discharged Emily in time for us to both be home at seven, shortly before he woke up.

Clearly he knows something has happened. Having him in the house has been a real blessing. His world did not stop spinning, as mine did. Though he is showing signs of stress, he is still concerned with trucks.

Emily is doing great. I think this is a bad sign. Physically, she is going to be o.k., but I don't think she has begun processing anything. She spent all day Wednesday looking for answers and has begun to blame herself.

As for me, I still don't know. I have had to hold my shit together for her and for Thomas. I am always the mission oriented savior type. I could not save Abraham. My little boy. I had to save his mother.

Last night a huge oak tree fell across our drive. It was not a tremendous storm, but the tree was large. We were home when it happened, but did not discover it until after dark when we needed to get to the store to buy food and medical supplies. I parked the car by the tree and worked for an hour or so with the chainsaw. Soaked, freezing and exhausted, I felt momentarily useful.

If or when you talk to Emily, please don't encourage her to relive the moment. I know that is painfully obvious, and not something any of you would be inclined to do. But keep her from it.

Once, a lifetime ago, I cut my thumb on a broken glass at a pizza restaurant in Atlanta. It was a bad cut and my first reaction was to jump up from the table and run into the kitchen. Thankfully my friend Julie was there and she drove me up to the ER at Emory. I don't really care for needles and blood. Julie held my good hand, pulled it away from me, and made me listen to some silly stories. And it worked. I didn't pay any attention to the stitches.

Hold Emily's hand. Tell us some stories. We are not, by any means, the only ones who know grief.

If you are the visiting type, or are close, we'd love to see you. Everyone's always welcome.

David

David Higginbatham, 37
Virgina

At Dawn He Takes My Hand

    The fetal monitor's saying
    Katy's playing
    It's thumping scores her ride
    She dives and surfaces
    the other side
    Her flutter kicks are whispering
    along my walls
    and down the halls
    and down the halls.

Whole fields of irises are blooming
I am rising on the wind
This is the Valentine I never sent
This is the hand.

    The bubble stirs and rises
    slips between a rock
    and the wall of the cave
I am glowing in the street
    The membrane ruptures
Water falling on my feet.

Midnight
Mother, almost mother,
praying
    Katy's playing
    unaware
    certain of my care
    she circles in the dark
    her fish eyes dreaming

In the next room
Mrs. Ramos screaming.

At dawn he takes my hand
They dynamite the door
I am not listening
for her dying
I am Demerol and crying

I am long and white and grieving
　　Katy's leaving.
　　Katy's fins are small
　　She swims against the tide
　　to stay inside, to stay inside
　　Her new ears deafened by the storm
　　she cannot hear the cries
　　she loses way
　　she dies
　　She sweeps through me
　　into light.

We do not look.
They tell me it's a girl.
I was right.

　　We burn the dead that come ashore
　　They told me that before.

"I lost this baby 30 years ago, when I was 32. Two years later I had a healthy son, got divorced, remarried, had another son, and finally a daughter, who we also named Katy in honor of my lost girl. She just graduated from college and has been a great source of joy in my life. My life seems to have been blessed…hardly any really terrible times…but that time was certainly a low point. As I see it now, everyone loses sometimes; no one gets away without pain. It's the nature of life. I think that experience made me wiser, more compassionate, less hubristic. No, I was not going to be excluded for any reason from the slings and arrows of outrageous fate. It made me more careful too, and more appreciative of everything I had. And time does heal most wounds, though you think it won't at the time. "Keep an empty bough in your heart, and the singing bird will come"."

Gail Rudd Entrekin, 62
California

They Weren't There
(But Dedicated to Those Who Were)

They weren't there when Michael and I pulled into the parking lot on that brisk Saturday morning in early October.

The sun's rays glinted weakly off the car windows and side view mirrors. Not a wisp of a cloud scurried across the heavens. By Halloween, the Buffalo sky would look as though it had been white-washed, and right before Thanksgiving, the snow would start falling. It'd keep falling for the next five months.

Michael and I walked into the downtown clinic's lobby. He consulted a directory by the elevators.

"Fifth floor," he muttered.

With a ping, elevator doors opened, though neither Michael nor I punched the button.

As we rode upwards, Michael fumbled to hold my hand, but I folded my arms tightly across my chest.

Yet, in the waiting room, when he put his arm around me as we sat side-by-side on the upholstered couch, I collapsed into him.

They weren't there either.

Silently, Michael ran his fingers through my hair, a tangled mess of light brown curls and snarls. I was glad he wasn't talking, but I wished someone in the overly crowded waiting room was.

Women sat rigidly next to men, contemporary, urban American Gothics. Teenage girls sat with other teenage girls, trying to look interested in fashion magazines, but flipping dully through pages that promoted make-up, hair care products and exercise routines. One woman — she must have been around thirty — rested her head on the shoulder of a gray-haired woman and sobbed quietly. The older woman shushed comfort.

More people entered. Teenage girls with teenage boys. College-aged women, sometimes with college-aged men but more often with other college-aged women.

"Twelve, thirty-seven, nine, fourteen, sixty-four and seventy-six," a chubby, pink-faced blond in a baby blue jogging suit called from the doorway leading to the clinic's interior. With her wide, toothy smile, she looked as if she was welcoming people on a cruise ship.

When I signed in at the receptionist's desk, the woman behind the counter told me I would be identified by a number in order to protect my privacy. I was assigned forty-four.

"But we don't go in regular order," she said, "like one – two - three. We use a random order as another way to ensure confidentiality."

Numbers twelve, thirty-seven, nine, fourteen, sixty-four and seventy-six stood awkwardly. Some walked as if half asleep towards the cheerful, chubby blond. One hugged a girlfriend, whose head bobbed reassuringly. Another tried to kiss the teenage boy besides her. His eyes darted around the room while he played drums on his thighs. He gave her a quick nod before she left.

"Hi!" the chubby blond exclaimed, her voice filling the quiet room. "Follow me!"

The six young women were swallowed up as the door swished shut behind them. A bolt slid into place. For the moment, I felt safe.

There wasn't a window in the entire waiting room. I couldn't see the blue skies. Michael rubbed the back of my neck, gripping and squeezing the taut, sore muscles with his fingers. I tried to think — about the food shopping I had to do for the week; about the vet's appointment I had to make for our cat, Ligeia; about the paper that was due next week in my graduate seminar in Modern British Literature. I tried to concentrate — buy bananas and bread and cereal and cat food and lettuce — but my mind was like a cigarette lighter with too little butane fuel.

The now familiar cramps tugged at my abdomen.

"Sh, sh— it's okay," the gray-haired woman comforted the thirty-year-old.

"I can't, I just can't," the younger woman moaned.

Those sitting near them shifted and leaned away.

Closing my eyes, I focused on my pelvic region. It felt as if a hand was inside me, pressing and squeezing my womb, releasing its grip slowly only to press harder the next time, just as Michael was doing with my neck muscles. I didn't want to be here on this brilliant October morning.

"Nineteen, fifty-six, ten, forty-four, and thirty-nine."

Michael helped me to my feet. I started shuffling towards the door, but his grip pulled me back. Peering anxiously through the lenses of his glasses and cradling my face in his hands, he murmured, "I love you, you'll be okay, this is the right thing to do." Indifferently, I nodded, shrugged him off, and moved towards the chubby blond and the doorway. With her pudgy cheeks and soft, pink skin, I imagined her a cherub, the kind that floats bodiless in clouds on old-fashioned Christmas postcards.

"Hi!" she called to the six of us funneling towards the door. Up close, her teeth were badly stained, the front tooth broken and probing her bottom lip like a sharp knife.

We filed awkwardly into a small, cramped room, where old green and orange plastic chairs were scattered higgledy-piggledy.

They weren't here, either.

We clutched our purses, brushed imaginary lint off our sweaters, combed hair with our fingers, scratched our arms. An older teenager with glorious thick red curly hair rubbed emollient on her lips.

"Take a seat," the blond invited, sliding a latch on the door.

We obeyed.

Six of us crowed into the room. The beautiful redhead. The thirty-year-old. Me. An overweight teenage girl wearing black hi-top sneakers, her hair teased and sprayed so much, it stuck straight up from her head in "mall rat" style. Two college-aged women.

"Hi, everyone," the blond began. "I'm Sharon, and I'm your counselor. What I'm going to do first is explain the procedure to you. Then we'll have a group session to answer any questions and make sure each woman is ready for the procedure.

"Now the procedure is very simple, very safe and very sanitary. I mean," she giggled, "it's not like having an operation or anything. Having wisdom teeth pulled is more risky and complicated!

"First, the doctor will dilate your cervix. This can cause some discomfort, but nothing worse than menstrual cramps. After the cervix is dilated, the doctor will insert a tube, like a catheter, into your uterus and clean out the debris there.

"Any questions so far?"

"W-wait," said the thirty-year-old. "What do you mean by 'debris'?" She took a Kleenex out of her pocket and dabbed her dark eyes.

"Well, the, um...You see, what you have in you right now is a blob of tissue. A lot of blood and, well, um, some tissue!" She smiled brightly.

Except in my blob of tissue, there were tiny hands and feet and a heart that already beat.

The week before, when I was in the gynecologist's office, I studied a wall poster on fetal development. At twelve weeks gestation, the fetus has formed hands and feet and a heart that beats. Hands and feet and a heart that beats. I sang those words as if they were a child's nursery rhyme. I was in my twelfth week of pregnancy.

"But I've had a baby," the thirty-year-old persisted. "I've felt a child move inside me, listened to its heart beat on the fetal monitor. What do you mean saying it's a 'blob of tissue'?"

Sharon smiled tautly, her broken tooth looking as if it might slice her lower lip.

"It might grow into something that moves," she said, "but right now, it's just a blob of tissue!"

"Oh, I don't know," the thirty-year-old shook her head, while the rest of us picked at cuticles, chewed on fingernails, examined our hair for split ends. If Sharon said it was a blob of tissue in my uterus, a blob of tissue it was. It was much easier for me to imagine an ugly, bloody blob of nothing than it was to think about tiny hands, tiny feet and a tiny little heart that beat, beat, beat.

"Then you'll go into recovery," Sharon continued.

My head jerked up.

"Um, why recovery?" I asked.

"From the procedure," Sharon answered.

"Yeah, but why do we need recovery? I mean, can't we just leave after it's all done?"

"You don't have to stay in recovery long. It's really just a precaution — you know, in case there's a little bleeding or something. Thirty minutes tops! Then you can leave. By Monday morning, you'll be able to resume all normal activities. But," she cautioned, "you should rest tomorrow. Nothing strenuous."

The thirty-year-old let out a shaky sob.

"Now, I need to — oops!" Sharon glanced at her wristwatch. "Wow — we have to hurry! We're way behind schedule!" She smiled at us mechanically.

"Anyway, I need to ask each one of you why you've chosen to have the procedure. We want to make sure that each woman has given this choice serious thought."

"You first," Sharon said, pointing to me.

"Well, um, I'm a graduate student. So is my boyfriend. We, um, need to finish our degrees right now. Of course, we want to get married someday, but this isn't a good time for us to—"

"Good," Sharon interrupted. "I can tell you've given this a lot of thought.

"Next?"

The overweight teenager confessed she didn't have a boyfriend. She wasn't even sure who the father of the baby was.

"Blob of tissue," Sharon said. "Don't say 'baby.' It's not a baby yet."

"Oh," replied the teenager. "Well, anyway, I figure the baby — if it became a baby — would be kinda all messed up, what with all the drinking and partying I been doin'. You know?"

She looked hopefully to Sharon.

"Oh, yes, definitely! If you've been drinking and stuff, the baby would be deformed. In fact, you'd probably miscarry.

"Next?"

"I don't know if I'm doing the right thing," the gorgeous redhead admitted. "This doesn't feel like the right choice."

"Don't go by feelings," Sharon counseled, stealing a quick glance at her watch. "Think rationally. How old are you?"

"Eighteen. But so was my mother when she had me."

"Want to go to college?"

"I guess."

"Then you're making the right choice.

"Next?"

"I don't know, I just don't know," The thirty-year-old cried. "I had a baby a year-and-a-half ago, and I suffered terrible post-partum depression. It was so awful, my mother had to live with me and take care of my son for the first four months. I just dread going through that again."

"Then you've made the ri—"

"But I'm not sure this is the answer." The thirty-year-old lifted both her hands and looked around the cramped room.

"My husband doesn't even know I'm here," she confided to us. "He doesn't even know I'm pregnant!"

"That's alright," Sharon reassured her. "It's your body, your choice."

"I'm here because this is what my mother thinks is best," the thirty-year-old continued. "She remembers how depressed I became after the baby was born, and she doesn't want to see me suffer like that again.

"And," she laughed bitterly, "She doesn't want to take care of an infant as well as a toddler if I'm incapacitated!"

"Then it sounds best for everyone if you went through with the procedure. It's the fairest choice to make — for your son, your mother, and yourself.

"Next?"

The two college-aged girls raced through their explanations. They, like the rest of us, were declared psychologically fit for the procedure.

"It's a difficult decision to make," Sharon told us. "And it's important we know you've thought it through carefully and made an informed choice. Otherwise," her blue eyes scanned us sympathetically, "it would be unethical for us to allow you to continue past this point."

Sharon buzzed a second door in the cramped room. A thin, homely woman in her mid-forties appeared, dressed in a white nurse's uniform.

"You're late," she snapped at Sharon, and then she barked at us, "Follow me, ladies."

We followed her down a hallway of freshly buffed linoleum floors to a room that was like a community dressing room in a department store. The nurse smiled at us, but she was so homely, her smile came out like a constipated grimace.

"Quickly, girls, remove all your clothes and put these on." She handed us each of us a paper dress. "Ties in the front. Once you've finished dressing, go sit on the bench outside the dressing room, and I'll be by to get you." With an efficient swish, she was gone.

The six of us were alone.

Women are funny about dressing in front of one another. The more modest ones have a perfectly executed system in which one article of clothing is removed and another put on without revealing so much as a nipple or thigh. Others might hide the parts of themselves they don't like. They cover small breasts by curving their spines, slouching their shoulders and angling their bodies so only a side view is exposed. They keep large, dimply buttocks hidden by positioning their bodies so all anyone would see is a front view. They lengthen soft, flabby bellies by arching their backs and jutting out their chests.

Certain women, though, just don't care. They may be fat, they may be thin. They may have beautifully sculpted legs or shapeless extremities marked by cellulite. They'll toss off their clothes with casual aplomb, some indifferent to an outsider's glance, others expecting admiration.

Whatever dressing rituals we six might have engaged in were we in a department store fitting room or a college dormitory, we abandoned in the clinic's dressing room. We turned our backs to one another and stripped, removing jeans and sweaters, underwear and bras.

"Did she say if we can leave our socks on?" one of the college-aged women asked.

"She said take everything off," replied the overweight teenager.

Rustling in our paper sheaths, we placed our personal belongings in cubbyholes lining a wall of the dressing room — more than half were filled with stuff — and exited, as a team, to take our places on the wooden bench in the gleaming hallway. No one spoke.

They weren't in the hallway, either, just as they weren't in the dressing room.

This time I looked even harder for them, craning my neck so I might see in both directions, squinting my eyes to improve my vision. But I only saw the homely nurse striding purposely towards us.

"Let's go, girls," she called when she was about four feet away. "Follow me!"

And once again we did, while she deposited us, one by one, into closet-size rooms where vinyl covered examining tables angled in the center, metal stirrups attached to the foot of each.

"Wait here for the doctor," she commanded each time she directed a woman into a room.

"Wait here for the doctor," she said, closing each door with a furious bang.

"Wait here for the doctor," she said to me, and the door slammed shut.

I was alone in a room with an examining table, a stool, and a machine plugged in over in the corner. I didn't see a sink or any sterilization equipment. I didn't smell any of the familiar smells of a hospital or a doctor's office.

In this room, too, there were no windows. I hoped the blue skies weren't fading the whole time I was at the clinic. I dreaded the long Buffalo winters, the reduced amount of sunlight, the steely skies, the gusty winds blew so hard sometimes it looked as if it was snowing upside down.

Sitting stonily on the uncomfortable, unyielding examination table, I gazed around the room. Right where one wall met the ceiling was a tattered poster of a blue lake surrounded by plush evergreens. I lay on the table and stared at the poster.

It was deathly quiet in the room. I strained to hear any sound of life, of movement. Resting my head on the hard, vinyl-covered table, I closed my eyes and dozed. I stood beside a rushing stream in a darkened forest. The waters were gray and foamy, swishing and swirling with great ferocity as they crashed downstream. The forest was murky and the water dense, but still I saw my autistic brother's body tossed about in the stream. I watched in horror as he tried to free himself from the water's powerful siege. The churning waters carried him along towards a certain death. My sister appeared on a cliff opposite from where I stood. She kept calling to me to jump and save my brother. She couldn't do it herself, because the only way to enter the stream safely was on my side. She screamed as we watched our brother's head smash into a jutting rock.

"Save him!" she cried.

But I couldn't. I was paralyzed.

I woke up with a rapidly beating heart just as the door to the examining room crashed open. In hurried a nurse and the doctor, a man in his early thirties with an untended, scruffy-looking beard. The nurse's eyes were quick and lively. They danced all over the room while she chattered, "Hello! How are you? I'm Claire and this is Dr. Benton."

The doctor's eyes were red-rimmed and dull-looking. He sat with a heavy thud on the stool at the foot of the table.

Claire moved with swift efficiency, wheeling the machine from the corner of the room to the doctor's left side, arranging my feet in the stirrups, helping me slide down towards the end of the table so that my knees were bent and my vaginal canal was completely exposed and accessible to the doctor.

"Is it just the two of you?" I asked.

"Yes, honey," Claire replied, bemused. "Who else would be here?"

"Oh, I don't know," I answered.

I didn't really expect that they would be here, but I hoped at least one of them might.

I looked at the poster. It was terribly faded. Given the absence of sunlight in the room, how could it get so faded? Probably it had been recycled from someone's bedroom wall. The doctor spoke not a word but went straight to his work. With deft fingers, he began inserting instruments into my cervix to dilate it. The dull abdominal pains sharpened with each thrust of his instruments. While before it felt as if a hand was squeezing one of my internal organs, it now felt as if that very organ was being mercilessly mashed between two large powerful hands.

My uterus roiled inside of me. Shutting my eyes, I squirmed.

"Hey," the doctor muttered.

"Honey, you have to lie still. The doctor needs to dilate your cervix, and he can't if you keep moving around like that."

"But it hurts," I cried, tears streaming down my cheeks.

"No, it's just a little bit of cramping — like a menstrual cramp."

"I've never had a menstrual cramp feel like this!" I said, clenching my teeth.

"Hmmmm," Claire stroked my forehead. "Well, the cramps probably mean there's something wrong with the fetus. Like a birth defect or something. Try to stay calm and relaxed."

I nodded. My head was clammy with sweat. The pain took on a life of its own, a shadow that leaned over and embraced me, darkening my vision, forcing my breathing into quick, rapid gasps. I wanted to pray, as I did at the dentist's office when I feared the drill bit was coming close to hitting a nerve, but I didn't think God or His Blessed Mother wanted to hear from me at that moment.

The doctor grunted, and a fuzzy Claire bent over for a moment, then straightened up and returned to my side. A loud whirring filled the room, sounding like a dishwasher in the final stages of a cleaning cycle, when the dirty water is sucked away into the plumbing. The machine slurped and slurped while the invisible hands inside me pummeled and mashed my uterus cruelly. The noise married the pain, and I blacked out.

"Is there a Tricia in here?" Someone shouted.

My eyes opened. When I was a little girl, I read a lot of books about kids living in orphanages. All the orphans slept in the same large room where iron-framed beds lined the walls in orderly rows. I might be in one of those rooms now. Beds were positioned close enough to one another, I could reach out and pat the mattress on either side of me. Bodies — some in prone positions, others curled into balls — lay on beds under flimsy cotton blankets. I listened to moans, and sobs, and the grin-and-bear it advice offered by the four women who ministered to the bed-ridden.

"Tricia?" A woman in her late thirties wearing a blue scrub shirt and a pair of jeans called out. "Is there a Tricia in here?"

Raising my hand weakly, I said, "That's me. I'm Tricia."

Grim-faced, she moved towards me, passing beds filled with young women. I didn't see them in any of the beds, though perhaps one was hidden under the covers.

"There's some guy named Michael whose goin' nuts in the waiting room," the woman in the blue scrub shirt told me. "He wants to know if you're okay."

"H-how long," I gingerly propped myself up on my elbows. "How long have I been in here?"

"In recovery?" She asked, checking the chart at the foot of my bed. "Mmmmm," she consulted her watch. "A little over two hours."

"Two hours?"

"Yeah, well, you've been bleeding pretty heavily.

"Look," she said, dropping the chart so that it clanged against the bed. "This guy Michael is throwing stuff around the waiting room and carrying on like a lunatic. We'd call security or the police, but we don't need the attention. He's saying he's going to break down the door to find you. Whaddya want me to tell him?"

I sighed.

"Tell him I'm...okay. Tell him I'm fine. Tell him...he owes me lunch."

She bustled off.

But I didn't feel fine. I felt completely empty. Placing my two hands on my abdomen, I pressed slightly. Hollow. I lifted the thin blanket and peeked underneath. My buttocks rested on a square cotton pad stained fire engine red blood. The skin on the backs of my thighs was wet and sticky. Someone in the bed next to me moaned. Guiltily, I dropped the blanket to face the despairing sound. I saw a tumble of thick, luxurious red hair.

"Hey," I whispered. I didn't even know her name, though I never felt so close to another person as I did to her at that moment.

The gorgeous redhead turned to me and pushed her hair away from her face. I peered into her luminous green eyes.

"I will regret this day for the rest of my life," she said.

Closing my eyes, I shook my head vigorously.

"Oh no, don't say that. Please don't say that," I begged.

"It's true. I've done a terrible thing, and I will regret it the rest of my life."

I turned on my side and offered her my back, feeling a fresh stream of blood pulsate from my body. The woman in the blue scrub shirt hustled back into the room and approached me.

"I told him you were fine," she said, "but he's still pretty agitated. Time for you to go."

She pulled back the flimsy blanket, exposing my body and the stained cotton pad.

"Don't you have to check my blood pressure or pulse or anything like that?" I moved into a sitting position, waiting for the dizziness to pass before I put my bare feet on the linoleum floor.

"You just need your discharge instructions." She handed me a single clean Kotex pad in a cardboard box, and told me to buy a package myself and change the pad regularly. If heavy bleeding occurred or if I spiked a fever, I was to call the clinic immediately for an antibiotic. She scribbled the clinic's phone number on the cardboard box and sent me back to the dressing room to change into my everyday clothes.

I was done.

"How do I get back to the waiting room?" I asked an attractive woman in her mid-twenties who was strutting down the long hallway carrying an armload of files.

"What do you need to go into the waiting room for?"

"Um, well, I'm all finished here. It's time for me to go."

"Oh no, you don't go back through the waiting room. Didn't anyone escort you after you left recovery?"

"No,"

"Here, let me show you the way out."

"But my boyfriend's in the waiting room. He's expecting me to meet him there."

"Don't worry, honey. We'll get him. But you have to exit through the rear."

I followed her down the white hallway towards the glaring neon "Exit" sign. She pushed open the door, turned to me and said, "This way."

I stepped out into a larger hallway just as Michael rounded the corner. He stumbled towards me.

"Oh my God!" he stammered, wrapping his arms around me. "You were in there for so long. I didn't know what happened to you. No one would tell me anything. I kept asking if you were okay, but they said they couldn't give me any information."

We were interrupted by a loud thud. The thirty-year-old was curled into a ball on the floor, rocking back and forth, while the gray-haired woman sat beside her.

"It was awful! Awful!" She smashed her head into the wall.

"Sh-h-h-h-h-h," said the older woman.

"Let's go," I said. "I want to get out of here."

We rode the elevator down five floors and exited the lobby. The sun had already begun its westerly descent. The sky looked as if someone had taken a paintbrush, dipped it in white paint and then a little water to dilute the color, and stroked it across the heavens with a swift, light hand.

They weren't there when Michael and I returned to our apartment, and they didn't call or visit during the four days I lay on the living room couch, soaking Kotex pads with bright red blood, the pain in my abdomen making it impossible for me to stand or walk.

On the second day, my temperature was 102 degrees. I crawled to the phone, called the clinic and requested an antibiotic.

"What for?" The receptionist asked curtly.

The excruciating pain made speaking difficult.

"I — I have a fever," I croaked through dry lips. "I've had one for the past day. Temperature's around 102."

The receptionist let out an audible sigh of irritation.

"The doctor isn't here right now. You'll have to wait until he comes in and then he'll call you." She hung up the phone without a salutation.

Later that day, I crawled back into the kitchen where the phone was and called again.

"Please," I whispered into the mouthpiece. "I called earlier. I really need an antibiotic. I'm burning with fever, and I'm in terrible pain."

"The doctor will call you," the receptionist said.

I tried calling again that evening but the clinic's phone just rang and rang.

The next day I pleaded more persuasively.

"Please," I whined into the phone. "I was told to call the clinic if I have a fever. I have one." I said. A tide of pain washed over me. Blood trickled down my leg.

"Look, the doctor will call you! But he's very busy. You have to stop calling here."

"I need an antibiotic."

"Take a Tylenol," the receptionist said and hung up the phone.

I finally got the antibiotic the next day, when Michael called the clinic himself.

"You tell that bastard of a doctor to order an antibiotic now!" He yelled into the phone. "Or I'll come down there to make sure he does!"

I felt better once I got a few doses of the antibiotic in my system; my temperature returned to normal, and the pain lessened to what this time really did feel like menstrual cramps. I was still bleeding heavily, but the color was darker. Every so often, I discharged clumps of what looked like pieces of chicken liver.

When Saturday rolled around, I wanted to leave the apartment where I had been imprisoned for six days.

"Let's take a walk in Delaware Park," Michael suggested.

Delaware Park was a block away from where we lived. It was a plush, beautifully landscaped piece of property, a Buffalo landmark.

A wind blew in from Lake Erie, whipping my brown curls back from my face as we walked. The air was crisp. Old trees lining the street had lost most of their leaves, though a few brown and orange ones clung obstinately to branches. The sky was faded blue, and I could see the sun better than I could feel it.

Michael and I entered the park and strolled on its well-maintained macadam pathways. A recent frost killed the mums. Their cheerful floral heads stood stalk-like and refused to bob merrily in the breeze. Their colors were dulled, their pungent odors gone. The ducks were still around, though, and I was glad Michael and I remembered to bring a few slices of stale bread for them. I liked ducks, especially the handsome mallard duck with his green head that shimmered as if pieces of mica were embedded in it. While our walk was a little more than an easy stroll, I started to tire.

"I'm just going to sit here in the grass for a bit," I said. "You go ahead and feed the ducks."

I sat on the cold ground at the top of the hill overlooking the duck pond. My knees were pulled up to my chest, and I propped my chin on them while I watched Michael make his way down the hill, quaking and clucking to the ducks as he walked.

The weak autumn sunlight shimmered on his soft blond curls. Bending his lean, beautifully proportioned body, he held out a piece of bread to one of the ducks and laughed when the duck nearly nipped his finger. He turned to me and smiled, his blue eyes gazing happily in my direction. His rugged good looks and finely sculpted features were the finest the Irish had to offer. Michael was handsome, and sexy, protective, caring and strong. And I knew I'd never love him again as I once did. Pulling my knees back to my chest, I cradled my head in folded arms and cried.

They were there on Monday when I returned to my classes at the university. They were strolling in the hallways of ivy-covered buildings. They were engaged in animated discussions over cups of coffee in campus cafés. They were lecturing dynamically to open-eyed, curious learners. They were in counseling centers and health service offices.

But not all of them. Some were in courtrooms and law firms and working for national agencies. Others, you yourself have probably seen on television, giving speeches or marching in demonstrations. All of them, each in her strident way, fighting for the reproductive rights of the overweight teenager, the thirty-year-old, the gorgeous redhead. And me.

Ann E. Damiano, 53; New York

Miss Carriage

you took the wrong taxi
carriage to life, but wrecked along the way
glass slippers shattered and pink dress whitened
the stroke of midnight came too early
pumpkin vines wrapped to strangle
what I thought was destiny
I wish I could have felt you in my heart
the way you felt inside my mother's
but it wasn't meant to be – given life, but taken away
brown hair, blue eyes, green
fruit that never ripened
little hands that never held another's
fingers interlocked with my own
I will never know
my mother's child – my sibling
never seen
never breathed

Daniel Lassell, 22
Kentucky

Abortion

It was a gloomy day. My monthly cycle was nowhere to be found, so as I strolled through the store aisle by aisle searching for the *feminine product section* — there it was…a pregnancy test.

Although my period hadn't come, I wasn't expecting to make it home and have to face positive results. I was pregnant. The day my mate and me had been waiting for had come, yet the wrong time.

I remember balling into a fetal position letting tears soak my pillow…and just feeling all alone. And even when you have someone to share those feelings with, especially when it is a man — they just can't understand how painful letting go of something living inside of you, just is.

You do a lot of back-and-forth thinking, contemplating and wondering what to do? Am I making the right decision? Will I be punished for this decision? Will I be forgiven? Will I ever forgive *myself?*

It isn't until you arrive at the clinic that you realize you are not alone. There are women of all walks and cultures that are going through your exact feelings of confusion and frustration.

My husband and I had been trying to have a child for over one year — then we decided to take a break due to the recession and our new financial struggles. And just when we gave up, it happened.

Only thing was…we couldn't afford it… therefore had to let go.

It hurt.

Angie, 29
California

Fetal Demise

friday

my old man waits
outside in his pickup anxious
to get back on the road he worries
about speed traps the price of diesel
about having another mouth to feed
says it's my fault not being careful

the doctor doesn't look at me
tries to explain the test results
I stop listening after he tells me
I detect no heart-
beat there's nothing
I can do you'll have to wait
until after the weekend

I start feeling like maybe it is my fault.

when I get back to the vehicle I tell
my husband he's quiet drives as I cry
later he paces half an hour around the living
room then vanishes on a four day run

saturday

I prepare meals I do not eat
as I lay on the couch my live child rests
her head on my belly she grieves the baby
sister I promised I tell her god wanted her
for company his house so full
of empty rooms but by Jesus
I don't believe god cares
to have another child again

let alone worry about mine
after I put her to bed
I dismantle the crib

sunday

I fold maternity clothes box them
maybe I'll mail them to my sister-
in-law expecting twins this spring
I visit the grave of my mother who died
birthing me my father remarried for love
alone could not raise a child he feared
just as I did when my first husband left
me with a two-year-old

monday

after the school bus disappears
I sign in mock-maternal a cut-
out mother to a paper child

my canopic womb bleeds
the wound gives birth to silence
I ask to see her someone cradles
a doll baby in my arms the weight
nothing more than the universe
the face a portrait of peace
I will bury above my mother

tomorrow when my husband returns
he will watch for a signal I am ready
to continue life as usual he will be
at a loss will mistake my coldness
for mere grief

donnarkevic, 56
West Virginia

Good-bye Little One

Even though
    Your whole world was confined
        To your mother's womb,

You somehow managed
    to   reach   out
        with hands so minuscule,
          and touch
            us all.

Now, as your fledgling soul turns homeward,
    clasp
        this truth
          in your wee heart.

Though your time on earth was limited,
    our love
        for you
          was not.

Susan Norton
California

Grass from the Grave

She died too soon. It's a selfish thing to think, especially since I didn't know her. Very selfish. I still think she died too soon. Possibly too young. She was seventy-nine-years-old. Up until the last two months of her life, she pressed and kneaded dough, wiped flour on her apron, and made lunch for her husband every day when he arrived home from his store.

Ben would drive to his parents' house and visit with her. I imagined them sitting at the table: Ben sipped on his coffee and his mother served him some of her biscuits. Those biscuits. Ben loved her biscuits.

Mine will never be like hers.

If I've learned one thing from all of my relationships, no matter how great my recipe is it will never be as wonderful as my boyfriend's mother's meal. I make my lasagna with ricotta cheese. Ben and my father prefer it with cottage cheese, because that is how their mothers had made it.

No one is at fault for her death, except for maybe Ben and me. It's certainly not *his* fault.

Maybe if I had let him die her heart would've let her live. Maybe if I'd gone to my scheduled appointment in Winston-Salem … no, my soul would've died.

Last spring, Ben left his wife and told the rest of his family about his affair with a younger woman and his baby boy. Since then, his other four children slam all respect for him in the dumpster. His family closes the vault on him, me and the baby.

"My sister told me, 'You had nine months to tell us and you didn't. We have nine months to get through all of this.'"

What man wants to deal with two angry families and an emotional, pregnant woman all at once? I remember Ben and I had already settled drama with my family by the time he had to tell his parents, brother, sister and children.

One day his mother was in full health, and then she dies. Ben's brother and sister request I not come to the December funeral.

Now the baby crawls, stands, claps and giggles while she rests in her grave. Today, the soft dirt covering her body will hold him up. It's the only time she'll carry the weight of the grandson she had never met.

I pull in to a downtown parking spot. The main street is split in the middle by train tracks. Although the railroad station is long gone, small town commerce of the mid-twentieth century etches itself in the bricks of flat top buildings. One of the last stores to carry local-made clothes hides in between two cityscape trees. For decades, millworkers had spun yarn and made clothes for the town, but with the decay of the economy and business moving factories to China and Mexico the small two-window shop is all that remains.

I remember the coffee shop as my favorite place to sit, drink a mocha *crappichino* — as Ben calls them — perform my interviews or write one of my stories for the town's newspaper.

These days, I'm a homemaker and at-home writer pulling my son's stroller out of the back of my green Ford Escape. It still shows the stickers of my college girl past. A faded pink Palmetto tree and quarter moon peel off in the corner and my University of South Carolina parking sticker is plastered on my back window.
The stroller weighs the amount of two, four-month-old twins.
God, I'm clumsy. I should've parked behind all of the buildings. There isn't a clear walk way downtown. I know that.

I wait for the traffic lights to turn red, and I push my baby across the street to the flower shop. Pink and white dogwoods bloom all around us, and a man cleaning windows tells me he hopes winter doesn't return. The ground hog had been wrong, he says. After all, spring arrives in late February on the border of the Carolinas.

I still feel like a newbie American spy in Russia. The bureaucratic government — just a fraternity of former KGB members — sends someone to watch me.

There isn't anyone with big, black binoculars hiding on top of buildings.
Come on, I say to myself, *not many people in this town remember me.* I had only worked for its hometown newspaper for a short time.

Most likely no one remembers me. Still, my heart beats faster, nerves crawl up and down my spine like spiders, and I'm aware many natives know Ben and his family. His father had opened his own store in the late 1960's, and now his younger brother runs it.

Outside the flower shop, a woman, with a crop of white hair, talks in her mechanical voice and yellow throat tube to a larger lady. I notice from my former work experience as a small town journalist many rural areas had lost their businesses. But here, people walk up and down the street on a sunny day, and there is talk of more restaurants to come and fill up vacant buildings.

I feel as if I enter a rich grandmother's parlor. Flowers in beautiful white vases decorate every corner. They're everywhere, like waiters at a restaurant ready to serve you. Plants make me nervous. They always die in my care. I usually forget when to water them.

In the first grade, I remember everyone's plants grew faster than mine. My brown stem remained a short, brown stem.

"How may I help you ma'am?" the lady at the counter asks.

"Yes ma'am, I ordered some roses yesterday."

"Of course, I have them right here. Would you like a card?"

"Yes ma'am, please," I reply.

She places two bright red roses wrapped in green paper and a red ribbon on the counter. I wish I had ordered something larger, but I don't even know the difference between flowers one buys for a wedding or a funeral.

"Sometimes simplicity is better," Ben had said to me.

I also wonder how I'll keep the roses on the grave. While it has warmed up, wind kicks up a notch blowing my hair in every direction. Ben will meet me in a little while, and he'll know how to keep them in place.

The lady hands me the card.

I write … *What do I write? What can I write?*

Ben's sister visits their mother's grave once a week. She'll see them, and I wouldn't want to upset her. She's already upset enough with her brother because her second husband had left her for a younger woman.

Dear Grandma, I love you very much, and I know you will watch over me from heaven.

Love, James

After the lady pins the card to the ribbon, I place them on James' stroller. Cars rev and run up and down the street. I guess school had let out early. A few teenagers race a jeep through all three lights.

It reminds me of Ben's two older sons: one away at college and the other embracing everything high school offers. Freedom. Freedom from boring adults and a father they probably believe has abandoned them.

"Neither one will pick up the phone or return my texts," Ben says.

My heart swells. I want to cry. As with his mother, I know there isn't anything I can do. The only thing I could've done to save the boys and Ben's mother from the truth is to have gone to Winston-Salem.

Ben would still have his other two boys.

I hurry across the street. The wind blows the roses off the stroller and they fall on the ground. I pick them up and make sure every petal is in its place. Petals are so delicate like butterfly wings. It's a fearful beauty. Once one touches it, and a petal; a wing breaks apart. I don't want to divide any sector from its creation.

James laughs and giggles as he swats his green frog rattle hanging on his car seat.

"Eeee-he-he agagaga," he says.

I am so thankful that I hadn't gone to Winston-Salem in October 2009.

My father always says an abortion is between the girl, her doctor and God. I believe every woman deserves the right to make her own choice.

While I drive to the cemetery, I remember thinking it was my only option.

As a journalist picking up the wine bottle more with every accident — deadly or not — I had grown sick of myself. Sick of right wing nut jobs who blame people like me for America's problems. Tired of pretending to love a jealous and angry husband who always cornered me. I think sometimes I should've done something else. But, I'd already spent years enough writing everyone else's story. The time had come for me to walk in the footprints of my own story.

"You're going to get rid of it right?" my ex-husband said to me. "Right?"

I left my sexless marriage, and the job I once longed for. My college friends dropped me like a penny in the sewer, and hell opened its jaws.

"When we do this," Ben had said me, "it'll be us against the world like two men in a bar fight. I'll have your back and you'll have mine."

I park my car on a hill. Ben pulls in behind me and carries James to his mother's head stone. An early spring breeze picks up throughout the cemetery.

"They didn't put those roses in a vase of some kind?" he asks.

"This is what they did. I guess I should've asked for one."

"It's okay. If you hold him, I'll find something."

When Ben returns from his car, he bends part of a clothes hanger and forks the roses at the foot of her grave.

I sit with James beside her flat grave marker. I pull out my cell phone and take a picture of the family — James playing next to his grandmother's headstone. The phone camera captures the late afternoon sun as it gleams over the baby boy and his grandmother.

James puts grass in his mouth and I catch it. He giggles and taps the ground like it's a judge's desk.

"He's got her red hair," Ben says.

I never thought I'd give birth to a red-head child. Maybe that's God's sweet vengeance on me.

"Well James, this is your grandmother," I say, *whom you could've met had her heart held up.* "I bet she loves you very much."

That's a strong gamble. I don't have anything to bet with except Ben's promise she does love James.

I didn't mean to cause you this pain, I say to her. *I know it wasn't right the way things happened, but I love your son very much. Ben's a great man and father and James is a good baby.*

"Soon," Ben says. "The rest of them will come around soon."

His mother was coming around *soon* to the idea to meet her youngest grandson last fall.

Soon crashed like a mythical star from heaven into the ground.

"Yeah...I hope so." James gurgles and picks more grass on her grave.

> "My mother struggled for several years to conceive a second child. The fear of not being able to conceive myself scared me. When I became pregnant in very different and unplanned circumstances I was very scared. I had an abortion scheduled until my doctor informed me about how many women suffer and struggle. I decided to keep my son. I don't regret it. This opportunity helped me find peace with my decisions."

Rebecca T. Dickinson, 25
South Carolina

My Baby

I love you, and we haven't even met.
People are talking about you
delighting in you
and they don't even know you.
We have never spoken,
but your heart beats next to mine.
Since you have existed,
I feel very fine
better than ever
and my love for you
will be forever.
I anxiously wait to see you
to hold you close to me
to feel God's holy promise
from your heart's sincerity

Krista Wagner, 35

Wanted

I wanted you before I thought,
you would ever exist even though,
I never expected to exist much longer myself.
You were more than a happy accident,
in my eyes you were all I ever wanted,
that I could never express in words, to even myself.

I wish I could say how well I remember the day.
We both know how my memory is just shit,
but I have a memory, broken images and feelings,
I remember the waiting, I remember hearing the news.
Most of all I very vividly remember the walk to the car,
how I felt, so happy and so careful about how to show it.

I wanted you before I thought,
you could possibly exist in a world like mine,
a world where 21 would never happen let alone next year.
I knew who you would be and I was ready for you,
no matter how young or unprepared I was at the same time.
I was ready to do whatever I had to do for you and only you.
In an instant you became my everything, my world, my very life.

At first I was alone but soon my world became our world,
I began to shape your life in my mind and build dreams for you.
Reality invaded and life intruded on all my plans and I did share
you.
I resigned myself to what I thought was best for you and I did
stumble, sometimes I did falter and I made so many mistakes but
always, you at the heart of everything, you always what mattered
most.

I wanted you before I knew how delightful you would be,
I wanted you before everyone else did, even though,
I wanted nothing else, I wanted you, I wanted you so much,
you were gifted to me despite the fact that I've never deserved you.

Sometimes I think I wanted you so much that my sheer wanting,
wanted you into existence,
just so I could share all your beauty and light,
with the whole wide world so everyone
can know the joy you bring me.

> "I never thought I'd be brave enough to share how I felt when
> I found out I was pregnant 16 years ago. I was so scared but so
> happy and thanks to you I have a chance to share that."

Jennifer Ann Hildenbrand, 34
Michigan

Heartbeat

After almost four years of trying to become a mother and three miscarriages, I was pregnant again. I had reached my tenth week — the furthest I'd ever gotten. My husband and I were renting a three bedroom house that looked over the San Gabriel Mountain. It was January of 1994.

Mark and I had met when we were both working at a labor union. I liked that he was shy, and I liked his voice when he spoke to me, but most of all what I liked was that he wanted to have a baby. At age thirty-three, after two abortions; I was feeling the passage of time, but something else too: a tiny shred of fear that I might not get another chance.

I had seen Mark lose his temper in a union negotiation once, but it wasn't until sometime after my second miscarriage that he got that angry with me. He had disappeared one night and didn't call. When I questioned him, he screamed at me and raised his fist. But after it was over, and he told me he'd go to counseling, I felt comforted when he sang "O-o-h Child things are going to get easier, O-o-h things are going to get brighter."

The first time we'd tried to conceive our child, I'd gotten pregnant right away, no problem. When I called Mark to tell him the news, he told me his car had just been repossessed.

A few weeks later, I met my friend Lisa for lunch. In the ladies room I suddenly felt wetness going down my leg. Bright red blood.

I had my second miscarriage two months later. The doctors still told me there was nothing wrong, but I was scared. By the time I got the news of this fifth pregnancy of mine — the third with Mark — I felt hopeful, but I wasn't telling people anymore about being pregnant.

I knew from my reading that I should be hearing a heartbeat by this point. At my January checkup, I watched my doctor's face as he placed the stethoscope on my belly. "If we don't see a heartbeat when you come back", he told me, "we'll have to think about the next step."

For two weeks I walked around worried I was carrying something dead inside. "There's nothing you can do," Mark told me, impatient.

Back in handsome Dr. Carter's office again, with my feet in the stirrups, I suddenly heard a sound "Isn't that a heartbeat?" I asked. My first one.

My doctor didn't look as happy as I was. "I'm not so sure about the size of the sac," he said. "Come back in a week."

It was the night before my next appointment. Mark and I were arguing again. I ran outside. He pushed me towards the door in front of the house. He said he didn't want the neighbors to hear us fighting. He called me bitch. He threw me down. I went to bed worried that the baby might not be ok after hitting the cement.

Next morning, I woke just as the sun was coming up, eager to get to the doctor. I wanted to hear that heartbeat again. I tried not to think about the night before.

Mark was still dead asleep. I stretched my arms. That's when I felt it — a sudden jolt, as if a car had hit the house. Then came the rocking and shaking. We were having an earthquake. I grabbed Mark and hung on. Finally the ground stopped moving. "I need to check our wedding china," I said. It was still not put away. I climbed out of bed. The room began to move again. Two pictures fell down. I heard glass shattering. I thought about the heartbeat.

The bed rocked again but not as hard this time. I waited. Mark said "I think it's stopped now."

I went first to the kitchen to see if the Mikasa was intact. "Hey put your shoes on!" Mark yelled at me. There was glass on the floor.

We drank decaf and tried to get a radio station to come through.

From up on our hill, everything was still now, as I dressed for my doctor's appointment that felt so important to keep. But suddenly I began to wonder what had happened down below. Many years before, I'd been in Mexico after their big earthquake. The morning after the quake, my friend Ramon had headed out to his job as usual — having slept through the worst of it. It was only when he headed out into the world that he understood the extent of the devastation. His building had collapsed; colleagues dead.

Now Mark and I were driving up the 2. The roads were empty. I heard sirens coming from all directions. Mark moved the radio dials for news but I wasn't really listening. I had to know what had happened to my baby.

When I walked in to Dr. Carter's office, I saw file cabinets on the floor and papers scattered.

I put my feet in the stirrups. The doctor spread the sticky gel over my belly. He moved the Doppler around.

No heartbeat.

They sent me over to the hospital — Verdugo Hills. I used to love the view from there. It's where I always imagined having my baby, looking out over the hills and nursing after my delivery.

When I woke up after the D & C, it felt like a pole had been stuck down my throat. As I went down the elevator, the door opened, hugely pregnant women in various stages of labor got on and off. I looked down at their stomachs and sobbed. One of them got on and our eyes met. She crossed herself.

I went home. My cousins Howard and Solita called. The apartment building where Howard's mother lived had collapsed. His mom was missing. They wanted me to help them look for her.

For several weeks people kept calling me and asking me how I was doing. Over and over, I heard the question: "What was the damage?" It took me a long time to realize that what they were asking about was the Northridge Earthquake.

Carla, 52
California

Saving Lives

I was somewhere around nine years old when my mother told me the story of how my father had raped and beaten her the night that I was conceived. She told me that the first time he had done this (raped her into pregnancy) she had aborted the child and that the doctor administering the abortion had made her feel so terrible that she couldn't bring herself to go back to do it again for me.

Despite how much more difficult her life was with me, and the beatings that continued throughout her pregnancy, she gave birth to me three months premature and with severe breathing issues that forced the first six months of my life to be spent in an incubator as well as a plethora of doctors visits, shots, and prescriptions that the money was scarcely there for following my homecoming.

Growing up, at times when she was inebriated, which were plentiful, her resentment was obvious in her words and actions, all of which caused me to develop pretty severe issues with attachment, depression, and guilt. It's not necessary to go into them in any depth as long as it's understood that they were there and bad enough to lead me towards a couple attempted suicides and many hours spent in contemplation of it, starting at the age thirteen. Now, at thirty years old, I look back at what I have done that has been worthy of the life that was given to me, and fought for by my mother, and I can say that I have saved people (including my mother) from drowning, initiated the steps that saved my step dad from death on our living room floor from heart failure and even managed to be the late night ear or emergency call to 911 that has saved several friends and even a few strangers from their own suicidal attempts or thoughts.

I know that the easier choice from the start would have been to abort, at times I admit that I have even wished that she would have, but because of her decision, who I have become through all of it because of her story, and what that has been for some of the people that I have come in contact with, all I can be is grateful to her and to the man who was despicable enough to make a strung out and abused woman feel even worse than she probably already did so that she could choose to deal with her consequences and fight, even if she didn't know that that was what she was doing.

This story, my story, I hope can show that despite how much more difficult the choice can be, sometimes it's the pain and struggle that we can choose to take on that can give us the perspective to impact the people around us the most positively and maybe even save our own lives.

Ryan, 30

The Life of a Teenage Mom

Raising a baby at 18 isn't that bad…right? How hard can it be? I baby-sit for my sister all the time. Well at least that's what I thought.

In November of 1994 I sat in my sister's bathroom — trembling with my pee stick in my hand. Waiting for what felt like a century for the line to show up; the double blue line showed up nice and bright. I called my sister to the bathroom to look at it and tell me what she saw. YEP it was positive — I was pregnant! What would I do now?

I was 17 years old in my last year of high school with many hopes and dreams. My boyfriend (who I thought I would be with forever) broke up with me a week prior as he felt "he needed to experience life more" — in other words — "he needed to date many women." I was devastated! I sat there in the bathroom of my sister's apartment wondering what my next step would be. Do I tell my ex-boyfriend? Do I tell my mom? Do I keep the baby? Are there any other options? It's amazing the thoughts that go through your head in such little time after finding out shocking news like that.

I thought back to what brought me to the position I was now in. I know exactly what brought me there. I was in love with my boyfriend and he convinced me to have a baby. He thought we would make a beautiful baby together and have this great life. He was 21 and I was 17. He was right about one thing; we did make a beautiful baby together, but if I only knew then what I know now…

The next 9 months were very up and down for me both emotionally and physically. I was living with my parents at the time and just finishing my first semester of grade 12. I was hoping to hide my pregnancy from my mom for as long as possible but that didn't last too long as I was very emotional and was soon very sick. My boyfriend (we can call him Jake) was put in prison for assault. After I told him I was pregnant, he was very angry with me and wanted me to abort our baby. I refused and felt that because we knew what we were doing at the time of conception it was our responsibility and I was going to take responsibility for our actions even if I did it alone. I will never forget that day. He called me over to his apartment and said he wanted to discuss "THINGS." He started off calm by telling me we were in no position to raise a baby and we were not even together any longer. I agreed but told him it wasn't fair to end a life because we decided to be irresponsible. This definitely upset him and he felt he had "NO" say. Jake told me I would be on social assistance and my life would never amount to anything if I kept this baby. He forced me out of his apartment…chasing me down the stairs…he pushed me but I managed not to fall. I ran to my sister's house; she called the police. My stomach hurt so bad that day, I was sure I was going to lose my child but fortunately I didn't. He was charged and put in jail for 30 days.

By the second month I was so sick to my stomach, the moment I woke up in the morning my head would spin and anything I ate came right back up. This went on until I reached 20 weeks or so. Jake was in and out of my life. He would call to see how I was doing but he was very angry as "I put him in jail." I felt very alone throughout my pregnancy; I felt ashamed. I couldn't finish my last semester of grade 12. I had applied to several different colleges. I was a smart kid with many goals but now had a setback. I was very worried about my future. I knew the next years to come would be very challenging.

I celebrated my 18th birthday in July — weeks before my baby was due. I had not finished high school and I was now living in a small apartment in preparation for my new baby to come. I spent every penny I got from social assistance on a crib, dresser, clothes, and other things my baby would need. Jake had his own place and spent most of his time partying while I sat and felt my baby's movements every night wondering what he/she would look like, if I would be able to provide a good life for him or her, if Jake would be involved or not??

July 29, 1995 — the BIG day! I had been experiencing a lot of cramping for two days prior after my doctor appointment. I knew the baby was coming. I went to the hospital that day with Jake and my mother but they kept sending me home, telling me my water didn't break and I was not in labour. I knew differently; every woman knows her own body even if she is only 18 years old. At

12:50 am on Friday the 29th my baby girl was born weighing 7lbs 5 oz. Her dad was there alongside my sister and my mother. It was a great day. The new beginning…

I had an apartment next door to my parents at the time. GREAT, they can help me out with the baby…right? Nope. Ashley was my responsibility and I didn't get to go out with my friends and enjoy myself. I had to stay home and take care of my baby. Her dad was there for one week and when he didn't like the fact that I wanted him to help me a little, as I was having sleepless nights and it interfered with his time for partying and having a great old time, he left. He would call and harass me every so often but didn't come around. We didn't see him for months. When Ashley was about 8 months, he decided he wanted to be a part of our lives again. We would stay the night at his place and he would get to know his daughter. I went through those sleepless nights and teething stages all alone. This had been so much more difficult than I had anticipated. I missed the prom. In fact, I didn't graduate. I spent many nights with a baby crying in my arms and a boyfriend calling to cause me stress…and now he wanted to be part of our lives?

When Ashley turned 1, my 19th year, when it's suppose to be the best time of your life — I worried the entire night while my mom kept her overnight as it was her first sleepover. My friends had me out in a bar and I barely drank because all I kept thinking about was the next morning and feeling crappy with a 1 year old running around…ouch. I was now 19 years old with a 1 year old daughter thinking about my next step. We lived in a nice apartment, Jake lived with us too. I finished my grade 12 that year with correspondence and decided to go through the program "Futures." This program would help me gain the confidence and experience to get out in the work force. I was placed in two different offices and was paid a little more than minimum wage. Ashley was in a home daycare and Jake worked odd jobs…Neither one of us had a driver's license. This made our lives even more difficult. We had to walk everywhere or should I say — I did. I would push my daughter in the stroller to the grocery store and pull her in a wagon and stuff it with as much groceries as possible as I couldn't afford a taxi cab.

By the time my daughter was 2, and I was 20, I decided it was time to go to college. Now that I had my experience working in an office I should have the education. I applied for office administration and Jake applied for some mining course. We were both going to start school in the fall. I was both excited and scared. I was now going to have Ashley in a regular daycare and she was only 2 years old but potty trained, which helped.

The next few years were so tough. I was without a vehicle or license so I had to drag my daughter in a sleigh during the winter and a stroller during the nicer weather to the daycare then walk to college which was probably four miles or so from home. I had a great friend at the time that was in college with me that had a son one year older than my daughter. Her boyfriend was great friends with my boyfriend. The only difference was — they were a great couple…the happy couple I wish I was. Jake moved in and out of our house several times within the next three years. We fought constantly. I was always caring for our daughter and he was enjoying college life. I worked during the summer at a restaurant and came home to take care of our daughter. I was worn out and very skinny during that time. He refused to grow up. He now had his driver's license but we didn't live together and he certainly didn't come to pick us up. We walked all the time (many miles on my legs).

By 2000 I had graduated from office administration and graphic design as well as other computer courses and some marketing. I had great grades and had a good foundation to find employment. Jake, on the other hand — finished one program out of the three years, was still partying and in and out of our home. I started a job as a receptionist for an insurance company. It paid $9.00 per hour. We lived in a townhouse — Ashley was now starting pre-kindergarten. I tried my best to give her what she needed but times were tough. I had to start thinking more about our future. Did I see myself spending the rest of my life fighting nonstop with my boyfriend? Will he ever stop doing drugs and now selling them? I made a decision to buy a house. I had saved all my money from my income taxes for two years and we bought a house.

I thought this would help Jake grow up and we would be a family…a normal family that our little one deserved. If I only knew what was yet to come...

The year we bought the house I also started studying to be an insurance broker as the company offered it to me and it would give me more opportunities as well as a pay raise. I started studying at home which was difficult with having a six year old and a boyfriend who didn't come home until the next morning or afternoon sometimes. I spent most of my time worrying about him rather than studying. That year was really a blur to me. There were so many tragic events in my life. I found out I was pregnant which was supposed to be a happy moment but with the way my boyfriend was treating me, I wondered if I made a mistake. I was still studying for my insurance license at the time. My daughter and I witnessed something horrible at that time. We were on our way to meet friends for a walk and witnessed a woman being killed by a vehicle, it was an accident of course but I saw it happening and tried to stop it. I was not successful and the woman died. My daughter ran and hid behind a vehicle and saw everything. Ashley was only six at the time. Things just got worse for us. My best friend found out her son had cancer — he was only 18 months. I lost the baby and my friend lost her son to cancer that year. I just felt like everything was crashing down on me. I failed my exam for the insurance broker. I didn't let it bring me down. I kept my chin up, studied and booked my next exam for three months later and passed! I tried to be the best support to my poor friend who was grieving the death of her 18 month old. She was an inspiration. If she was about to pick up the pieces and keep going, then so should I. That year made me think long and hard on where I was and where I wanted to be. After seeing my friend go through her tough time and seeing how she and her husband survived this time and stayed a strong couple, I knew I was with the wrong person. I had no support when I witnessed a woman dying, I had no support when I almost lost my own life, when I lost my fallopian tube due to an ectopic pregnancy, and I never had the support you should have when you are a strong couple. I had to make a very tough decision, one that would affect myself and my daughter very much........I left.

I didn't only leave him but I left the town I grew up in, I left all my family and friends, I left the house that I had grown to love —

the one I bought with my own money. I took a job in Niagra Falls, Canada. It wasn't for very much more than what I was making at the time but it was going to get me away from all my troubles. My sister lived 20 minutes away from where I was moving. I found a nice apartment with security and my job was down the road because at this point I STILL didn't have my license. I had my G1 but didn't go for the G2 as Jake made me feel like I would never pass and he didn't have the patience to take me out driving, so I just didn't go.

I was now 25 years old with a seven year old daughter — single, 9 hours away from home from everything I have ever known. I knew no one in the building or the city, my daughter was starting grade 2 in a new school down the street where she knew no one and we were both scared to death. I questioned myself many of times if I had made the right move?? Could I have just broken up with him? NO it was no longer an option — I had tried and he always manipulated me to taking him back, he had become a very angry person with the use of drugs, I was now afraid for mine and my daughter's life. I do believe I left at the right time now thinking back. I was so scared that one day the police would show up as he was taking part in illegal activity and they would take Ashley from me as they would feel I was unfit. She was my whole life; she was the reason for everything I did. I was tired of being scared. I was tired of spending sleepless nights wondering what kind of mood he would be in when he got in the house IF he came home at all. I was tired of my daughter being so afraid, she would clutch on to me all day long. She didn't play like a normal child would of her age; she wanted to protect her mom.

We struggled for a good year to make ends meet. My job didn't pay much more than my last one, my house was rented to a friend and she was paying me just enough to pay the mortgage and tax bill. I was paying the utilities. I had to do something. I had now met some friends and was doing great socially and had some great emotional support, but financially, I was barely keeping above water.

A year later, I switched to a different office that doubled my salary. I lost my house but was starting over. Jake was not paying support. I believe he was in and out of rehab. Ashley was now going into grade 3 and we were moving yet again. This move again was for the right reason. That winter I promised my daughter I would have a license and I kept my promise. I got my driver's license in May of 2004. We had a crappy little car but it got us from point A to point B and that's all that mattered.

It is now 2008 and I am still at the same employment — making triple of what I was making when I first started out, my daughter is going into grade 8 — she's healthy and beautiful. I am with my perfect man and we bought a house this past March. I am 31 with a 13 year old! CRAZY. Her dad hasn't seen her in four years.

I know that life could have been much easier but this was the path I took and I made the best of it. We start off life thinking that it will go a certain way, but you never know what bumps you will run into. I have experienced so much and learned so much that I have no regrets! I believe we are thrown curves all the time and we are tested more than you and I know it but it's how you handle it that counts. We are so much stronger than we think. The challenges I overcame made me who I am today and will make my daughter a stronger person. It breaks my heart that my daughter had seen and experienced some of what she did, but I think she will understand some day that I tried my hardest to give her the life she deserved and that the outcome was pretty good. She knows the value of life and has learned a lot from me. I went many years with my head down carrying my baby as I knew what others thought.

They thought I was another statistic, a teenage mom who would never amount to anything, but after everything I have gone through; I think some of those moms can learn a heck of a lot from this teenage mom! My life may not have been the "ideal" life with the choices I made but it is my life. I am NOT recommending being a mother at 18 years old, it wasn't easy, but you do not have to be another statistic if it does happen. Unfortunately, we do not start off life knowing everything we later find out. We will all make choices that may not seem right to others and be frowned upon for it, but the important thing is you learn from it. I have to bow down to any young single mother out there; your job is not easy but keep your chin up as it does get easier with time and the reward is awesome!

"So much has changed in my life since my daughter was born. I am now married to a wonderful man and working on extending our family. I have a successful career and my daughter is now almost the same age I was when I gave birth to her. I believe that my experiences (good and bad) have helped me become who I am today. The choices I made almost 16 years ago have helped me appreciate life in so many ways. I am now faced with infertility which makes me very thankful that I made the choice to have my daughter even though I was 17 years old."

Cindy, 33
Canada

My Unborn

To my unborn children-
the first three lost before
the others began to crest
fully formed, and one more
half-way through the parade
of four we welcomed,
before interrupting the process
due to advancing age
and full hands, yet I always felt
there would have been
another girl otherwise,
after the last, had we not
taken that step, but seldom
have I devoted much
consideration to those others-
four more who would have
brought joy or grief, four
who would have failed
and succeeded, cried and
giggled, four who might have
broken the lap or back
or quiver, or elated it in
measures I cannot comprehend.

> "Raising our four children has been the single most gratifying
> investment of my life. Loss, trials, effort, and exhaustion
> prompted prayers that forever changed my life with joy."

Dianne Silvestri

Gorgonzola

Sally pushed the cart forward, turned the corner and hit another's shopper's cart while trying to read her shopping list. She looked up, saw her neighbor Millie, now struggling to maintain her balance, clinging to her shopping cart.

"Sorry Millie!" said Sally.

Sally rushed over, put her hand out to support Millie. Millie, the white haired woman wearing bifocals and a cherry, red sweatshirt she got for Christmas ten years ago, refused to take her hand. She looked at Sally with a scowl, taking a moment to recognize her.

"You trying to kill me?" Millie asked. "I said I'd give you that money for the snow plow. Just waiting for my check."

"I know. I know. I was just looking down at my list. Are you okay?"

Millie looked at Sally, frowned.

"I'm fine. I didn't think I'd get dead buying groceries. Watch where you're going!"

"I will. I'm so sorry Millie."

Millie softened.

"Just what's so interesting on your list anyways?"

Sally sighed, glanced at her paper. "Gorgon.....zola cheese?"

Millie grabbed the list from Sally's hand.

"What do you want to do with something that fancy?" she asked.

Another shopper approached, but couldn't get through. Sally moved her cart to let her pass.

"Oh, I don't know. Special dinner for Phil. He's been working so much lately."

Millie eyed the recipe with a skeptical glance then gave it back to Sally.

"Don't expect a miracle," she said, then walked away.

Sally watched her go, wearing an expression between hurt and confused, but much closer to hurt, and proceeded to the dairy section.

A half an hour later, Sally waited in the check-out line, crossing items off her list. The clerk, Diane is a mid-fifties, plump, pleasant looking woman. She started ringing up Sally's groceries.

"You having a party or something?" Diane asked.

Sally looked up, found Diane smiling at her.

Sally laughed, revealing a pretty smile on her thin, pale face.

"Can't a girl get away with anything in this town?" she asked Diane.

Diane laughed, shook her head no.

At home, Sally turns on the light in her already darkening kitchen. It's a small room, not terribly modern or updated, but with a clean, retro look. She checks the messages as she starts putting away four full bags of groceries, leaving out only the items specially purchased to make gorgonzola salad. She found the recipe on the fridge and placed it on the counter.

Gorgonzola Salad
- 1 teaspoon salt
- 1 teaspoon red wine vinegar
- ½ cup extra light olive oil
- 3 cloves garlic, crushed
- 1 head lettuce
- 1 ounce Gorgonzola cheese, crumbled

She decided to make the salad with barbecued beef sandwiches. Too much exotic wouldn't be appreciated by Phil. It wasn't necessary. Just a little thing. Make an effort. Let him know you care.

Sally wonders if the regular olive oil will work since she couldn't find the extra light. It should be fine but she has no idea how to crumble cheese. She should have bought it that way. How hard could it be to crumble cheese?

She started by moving the ingredients to the table, has to move the baby names book out of the way. She glances at it, she sees the yellow post it note on her favorite page. Her favorite page has the name Amanda. Maybe a dog. Maybe next year. The doctor didn't say never.

Music. Yes. She definitely needed music. Aretha. The ingredients didn't take too long to stir. Nothing too complicated. The cheese was easy to crumble. Yesterday she didn't get out of bed. But today was a good day. The salad was the right idea. She poured herself a glass of Chardonnay. It went down easy. It had been so long. There was no harm in enjoying the taste every now and again.

When the phone rang, it took her a moment to remember where it was.

"Hello?" she answered on the fourth ring.

"Sally? It's Phil."

"Hi."

"You sound good. Are you having a good day?" he asked.

"Yes. Very good."

"I have to work late. I'll be home around eight. You're okay right?"

"Mm-hmm," she assured him. She assured herself.

"I'll see you then," he said.

As she hung up the phone she noticed how loud the music was. He hadn't asked about it though, so it must not be bothering Millie next door. She turned it up and poured another glass of wine. Aretha was almost done. Put in another CD.

It was simple to make barbecued beef the way he liked it. He had a favorite sauce. Cook the meat. Add the sauce. She relished the smile on his face every time he ate it. She pictured his scruffy, bearded face. He was all man. He worked outside every day managing highway crews. He always looked slightly sunburned even in the winter. Handsome. Very manly. Was she woman enough for him? She sighed, knowing the answer was no.

"I'm tired." Sally said to herself.

She put the salad in the fridge, the beef in the crock pot on low.

"I need to lie down," she said to no one.

When she walked to the living room, it seemed dusty. Everywhere she looked, dust. When was the last time she vacuumed or used a dust mop? She couldn't remember. She looked at the clock. It was 7:30.

She knew Phil would be home soon.

I'll just lie down for a minute she decided.

When she did, she noticed the pictures of her niece and two nephews on the fireplace. They were so cute, so energetic, so red faced. Who told them she wasn't going to have the baby? Did somebody tell them? She couldn't remember. Hopefully somebody told them, she thought before she drifted off to sleep.

"Sally?" Phil asked.

He touched her shoulder gently, studied her face.

"Are you okay?" he asked louder.

She opened her eyes, saw him looking at her. He was blurry, but still handsome.

"I must have fallen asleep. Is it late?"

"It's eight."

He picked up the wine glass.

"Did you have more than one?" he asked.

"Maybe two."

"The doctor said you shouldn't drink until you're off those pills."

"Yeah, I guess I forgot."

He lifted a bag of food off the coffee table.

"I brought you some dinner," he offered.

"Your favorite bacon cheeseburger double deluxe with onions," he said.

When she inhaled, she smelled meat. It took just a moment for her eyes to adjust to being open again, to see the room with Phil standing next to her. She remembered.

"I cooked," she said.

"I can smell the barbecue sauce. We'll eat this tomorrow," he said, pointing to the bag.

"It's okay. We'll have mine tomorrow."

"I just figured."

"Yeah."

Sally hadn't cooked in six weeks. He had no reason to think tonight would be different.

"What else did you make? Not that the barbecue isn't enough. It's my favorite."

"Nothing special. Like I said, we can eat it tomorrow."

"Okay baby, if you're sure. Let me get you to bed, help you into your pajamas."

"I can do it myself."

"You sure?"

Sally wished she didn't remember why he considered her so helpless. But she hadn't done much of anything lately.

"Okay I'll get some plates. You want to eat at the table?"

Sally nodded, got up, headed for the bedroom.

"Phil?"

"What baby?"

"Did anyone tell them?"

"Did anyone tell who what?"

"Jen's kids. Do they know about the baby? Do they know the baby isn't coming?

"Yeah baby they know."

Phil entered the bedroom where Sally looked for a pair of pajamas. She couldn't seem to find them. He knelt down, opened the bottom right drawer, handed them to her.

"Next time the baby will make it. I'm sure of it. The doctor even said."

Sally took the pajamas, nodded at Phil, tried to smile. She caught a glimpse of herself in the mirror.

"How did I get so thin Phil? Was I always this pale?"

"No you're fine now. We're going to fatten you up. Get you in the sun. You're gonna be fine Sally. You're as beautiful as ever."

"They were going to put me in the hospital weren't they?"

Phil shakes his head, reached for her, embraces her, kisses her ear.

Sally thinks for a moment she's going to fall over but holds Phil and starts taking off her clothes, changing into her pajamas. Phil watches, lets her do it herself.

"You're not going anywhere now. Let's just eat."

Sally nods, thinks about what a good husband he is, how she could have lost him. But once he eats the salad, he'll know. She's a gem and he's going to keep her. She's sure now. He wouldn't leave her. Tomorrow she's not going to be so pale either. She's sure. Tomorrow will be another good day. They'll eat the salad.

Deanna Perchyshyn

A Better Night

tonight will be better.
I will awaken her
take her to the bathroom
an <u>hour</u> after she goes to sleep.
she wets so soon !
even if she pee'd right before bed!
even if she didn't drink anything after dinner!
even if....
even if anything.

" c'mon, sweetie, let's get to the bathroom…"
she, asleep like a turtle in winter mud.
I, arms under hers,
her stocky 9-year old body deadweight,
we lurch together to the bathroom.
I sit her down, the sleepwalked, the sleepsitting.

"okay, honey…. okay, sweetie… can you pee? time to pee
now…"
I stroke her tousled hair,
turn on the water in the sink,
await echoing tinkle.

I fight back swells of frustration,
at the divorce that left her so vulnerable,
stifle rage
that, dry at two years old,
most nights now bring a flood.
she, my little angel who has become
frighteningly conscientious and responsible,
who never complains on leaving for the weekend,
never throws a tantrum upon returning on Sunday
like her brother needs to do,
never seems to feel much at all anymore.
never lets me hold her.

but every night her levees are breached
every night the flood.

I'm grateful for her somnolence
on the toilet
while I wrestle with my demons.

tinkling of release.....ahhhhh.
"oh, good, honey, that's good."
we lurch back to her bed, she unawares.
I hope against hope that enough has drained off.
I will try to get her up again one more time
later in the night,
but often I am too exhausted to do so.
maybe tonight will be a good night.

not that washing the sheets is that big a deal.
it's just another load of laundry.
no, it's the *dance* that's hard:
she pretending not to feel bothered by the morning-wet bed
(or anything),
me pretending not to see
the tension around her eyes belying the lie;
me hoping she doesn't see the tension
around mine, damming my own spill;
me pretending to believe
that she believes me when I say,
"it's okay, honey, it's okay. don't worry":
she fighting the urge to run into my arms
like she used to, before;
me fighting the urge to wail my keening right out loud,
at the loss of my angel's innocence.

already 5 years into this ritual
this middle of the night dance.
it will continue until puberty sets in,
a mid-month flow will replace this mid night spill.

then the werewolf will strike,
the midnight hunger, canine and insatiable

it'll drive her to the fridge in the dark
shake her in its ravenous maws
until she eats the rest of the cake.
she will hardly wake up.

I will not be included in that.
I will left, up alone in soul's dark night
to howl down the moon of my powerlessness
to save her from pain
to keep the night away.

Jan K. Dederick, 64
California

My Son

My husband and I had been married for three years. He was no longer the man I married. The man I fell in love with was no longer there...He used to be sweet and do anything for my happiness, but then he turned bitter and resented me and our son. He made a comment that our son and I piss him off... Our son was two.

We went to marriage counseling but it didn't help. My husband didn't see anything wrong with his behavior. Sometimes I would stay up until three or six in the morning waiting for him to come home from wherever it was that he had been. We would get into fights that would result in him sleeping in a different room or he would tell me what I wanted to hear with no real intent of changing.

It was really hard to love him. He was no longer the man that I had fallen in love with. He no longer took my breath away and didn't want to change. I couldn't make him change. I knew in my heart that the best thing to do was to leave and that's what I did.

My mother didn't support me at first, so I moved in with my older brother, his wife, and their kids. My sister-in-law helped me with the paper work. We were all afraid that my husband was going to beat me or kidnap our son.

At that time, I felt like I was in the pit of despair. My husband didn't want the divorce and kept telling me that he was going to change. I knew it wasn't true, however. I had given my husband a countless number of times for him to change and I was so sick of crying until I fell asleep. I was so sick and tired of being married and raising our son on my own. It got to the point where my son would ask me "Where's daddy?" when I would tuck him in and I would have to say "I don't know." It's just so heart breaking to be in a marriage that only one of you is trying to make it work.

So I moved in with my brother and sister-in-law. I was still going to school and majoring in physical therapy. I finished my classes and passed, but before the next semester started, I saw that I would now be a single mother and I could no longer be a physical therapist because it would be too time consuming; and if I wanted to see my son at all, I would have to change my major.

After much thought and consideration I switched my major to massage therapy. Massage therapy only requires six months of schooling and most classes were at night. So that's what I did. I graduated college and got my vocational certificate for massage therapy in May 2010.

It was really hard being a single mother and going to college, but I know that my son is worth it. He is my life. He is my motivation. I decided a long time ago that nothing is going to stop me from being a good mother to my son and providing a better life for him.

I look back at this period in my life now and I realize that my husband at the time actually did me a favor. He showed me that I don't need a man in my life to be successful. That I could make it on my own and that my son and I would be okay.

> "The Help Inspire Others project means a lot to me because as a kid I had been through a lot. I have had a lot of trials happen to me at a young age and once I thought that death was the only way out. But then I discovered that hearing from others who have been through the same circumstances helped me and gave me strength. So that's all I want to do. I want to return the favor. I want others to read my story so that others will know that they are not alone and if they are going through the same circumstance maybe it will give them strength and advice to get through their trials."

Heather, 26
Florida

The Single Mother and the Long White Nightgown

It was there in the window
for seven dollars
It was there in the window
on the way to work
& it beckoned her,
it seemed to lead her on,
this long slim white nightgown
with thin straps to slip over her shoulders
& one sinuous long green stem
with green leaves
& pink & golden roses
stenciled down the front from bodice to hem,
a few buds scattered alongside it.
It was a gown sleek as a young girl's body
It was a gown to sculpture a woman's body
It was not lace, it was not pretense
It was all shape
It was chaste
& yet the roses on the long stem
& the way it clung, bespoke
sensuality
bespoke
the beauty of a woman's body.
It was a Monday morning.
She walked by that shop all week.
On Friday she walked in the door
& bought it.
Because it reminded her of the virginity
she had plucked & cast away
so long ago, casually
as a cut flower
& because it made her feel she was a virgin again,
&, this time, precious.
Because it reminded her of the man she loved
but could never have,

& it felt like his eyes loving her.
She wore it to imagine their wedding night.
She believed it because it existed in her heart.
In this way she managed to survive,
& give love to her children.
In this way she managed without a man's arms.

Karen Ethelsdattar, 74
New York

Miscarriage

I knew the moment you were here
And the moment you left me

Little sparkle traveling within me
Buzzing softly under my surface

Big plans we made for your arrival
That came too early.

Not enough time
Not enough development

Where have you gone?
Are you waiting somewhere in the darkness?
Will you come back to me?
Will I feel you again nudging your presence again?

It's been a year now since I've lost you
Since your body slipped from mine

I'm sorry I wasn't better
More equipped
A better mother

I pray to see the reason why this happened
I beg to understand the pain I've gone through
Was it another lesson? One of many to experience?

A different kind of birth has happened to replace yours
A new me has taken over – stronger and more creative
Someone who's been hiding for a long time....

Nothing gained could be enough to replace you
But somehow I am okay

I hope one day the conditions will be right for me to hold you
To Smell You
To Kiss You
To Make You Laugh

Until then I'll keep writing....

"My miscarriage was the hardest thing I've ever had to experience in my life. The hardest part of going through this ordeal was that I felt like I had let so many people down. I felt like a failure. It took a long time to forgive myself even though logically I knew it wasn't my fault. I thankfully had a very supportive family unit that made the pain easier to bear. Not everyone is as fortunate as I am. Since the miscarriage I've taken up writing again, something I haven't done in years. I needed there to be a reason behind the pain, something to emerge that would help make sense of what had happened and writing has given me that. From my loss I've gained a part of myself I'd hidden away and given up on. I think expressing yourself through words and through this project can be a huge part of the healing process after a traumatic or life changing event. I hope more people find this resource and find their voice. Writing my poetry has helped me and I believe it can help others."

Katie Josephine Gabbert, 29
Minnesota

How I Feel

I think I am ready to tell you how I feel. I am finally ready to share with everyone what this did to me and how I was affected each and every day. I remember sitting in your bed that night telling you I was pregnant, I can still hear the words that you said so tenderly and kind, and how they pierced me like a million little pins. "Do what the other girl did." I could feel each word sting my skin…millions of tiny pins stabbing me. I was hurt. I felt lost. I felt like my life was over. I was uncomfortable. I felt nervous. I was terrified. I felt alone…so incredibly alone. I felt angry. I felt overwhelmed. I felt numb. I felt torn. I was sad. I felt like a failure. I felt like no one would love me ever. I grieved the person I was the day before. I didn't have time to grieve. I felt empty. My stomach hurt. I couldn't sleep. I cried, daily. I knew everyone was staring at me. I felt weak. I felt foolish. I was alone with a growing belly. I felt like no one could hear me. I felt thrown aside. I heard people snickering about me in class. I felt disconnected. I started losing myself. I felt bitter. I was full of anxiety. I felt broken. Who would want to date me? How was I going to do this? I was young. I was out of sorts. I felt panic. I felt scared. I felt like I wanted to run away. I felt displaced. I wanted someone else with me when I got my sonograms. Someone to smile with. I wanted to hide. I felt afraid. I felt consumed. I wanted to scream. I was exhausted. I wanted someone to feel the baby move. I didn't like people staring. I felt abandoned. I wanted to hate you. I wanted you to understand. I wanted you to know what I went through for a long nine, draining, months. I wanted to call you to tell you it was a girl. I didn't want you to miss her birth. At the same time, I never wanted to see you again. I, for a moment, was heartbroken. How could someone just leave someone in a time like this? Easy for you I suppose. I have wanted to tell you how I felt about this for a long time. I wanted to tell you I thought you would have been a good father. I know you would have been. Deep down your heart loves her and I know it does. But that doesn't mean I don't hope you are tormented every night when you are trying to go to bed. I hope your heart suffers from your loss — of not knowing her. I hope you feel incomplete on Father's Day. I hope you are sorry, regretful. I hope you realize what you lost. I want you to know we have an amazing life. All those years of all those mixed emotions comes down to this. I am thankful everyday for the beautiful daughter I have to share my life with. I never thought it was possible to love someone as much as I love her. She has been given nothing but the best since the day she arrived. She is an amazing little girl…a little girl that you won't see grow up, you won't hear her spell, you won't see her dance recitals, you won't comfort her when she falls, you won't hear her sing, you won't know how smart she is. You won't know what parts of her belong to you. You will miss out on raising an extraordinary little girl. And the only person you have to thank for that is yourself.

Melissa, 27
New York

To My Unborn

baby I haven't

thought of how you were

inside of me

in some time.

when I lost the letters I wrote to you during advanced algebra

I don't know.

but I remember something about your

unblemished light brown skin,

something about

lullabies —

if there is a heaven and you are to be mine again will you be how I
remember you? it is because of this chance I left your father, this
you should know: your brief life was reason enough for me to go.

Marit Rogne, 24
Michigan

Troubled Blood

Their chill crystallizes
like frost on my bones.
The verdict:
pregnant and careless
of damaged kidneys
doing double time.

Doctor shakes his head,
husband's mask sets,
parents avert their eyes.
I slink off into myself
and burrow deep
against the stern silence.

A gathering of books
instructs my ripening,
sustains me fall afternoons.
Just before Thanksgiving
the well goes dry.
I am carrying spring water

back to the house
when I feel it,
a loosening, a gurgling down
of unbloomed life
in troubled blood
that lying down cannot stop.

A small burst of sorrow
gives up a trickle of tears,
enough to buy
the doctor's nod,
husband's smile
parents' words:
that's best.

"The underlying medical condition causing concern in this poem is Lupus, which I have lived with since 1982. At the time of the miscarriage, it was more active. I went on to have two children; and, though the second birth did cause serious kidney problems, they were brought under control by chemotherapy. I am glad I didn't allow fear to make me miss out on having children."

Susan Martinello, 60
Alabama

Nothing Planned
Nobody's Parenthood

In the waiting room
long faces sandwiched by dreary walls.
Couples sit hunched into each other
Whispering lament, day dreaming what if
mostly wanting to get it over with.
It's an end to a beginning.
A relief from the sickness,
exhaustion, and hunger,
that comes loaded with fear.
The wait is long.
They take you in then send you back
to wait.
Many times you waver
stare longingly at the EXIT.
My man couldn't take it, said the room,
the whole vibe was making him nauseous
he hid in the car passing hours.
I stay eyes wide waiting for impact.
Death
of cells
or death of souls?
My little bean shaped child
taking up some grey area
on the ultrasound screen.
No woompa woompa heartbeat
or tiny waving hands.
On the table I feel like meat
bloody butcher paper scrunched under
my bare shamed ass.
First we spread our legs,
get into trouble.
Then we spread our legs,
to get out.
The table is stained

like me
its seen a lot of traffic.
I say goodbye to a red lump
in an emesis basin,
feel all that's shitty
about being a human
about being a woman
about having choices
and not having options.
I don't know how these doctors do it,
set their teeth
and go about the work.
They tell themselves it's lifesaving,
and I'm not saying it isn't.
I'm just saying
I don't think
I'm the only one here
even more afraid
of the dirty feeling
than the pain.
Imagine days,
miles of regret.
Imagine children
that shine like a full moon,
like a heat wave in January
pure confusing sunshine.
Back here on planet earth
I'm hurtling along head fuzzy
on the exam table.
The decision has been made
and though he says he doesn't
hold it against me,
some days he describes
the bare feet on wood
sound of first steps.
The way they speed up
when they see you.
Little faces held close
the scent, the breath

of a tiny flawless you.
And he told me
after it was done
that he would have
taken the baby everywhere
gotten up every night,
even if it was all night.
But there is
no more baby
to wake us.

Cassandra Dallett, 39

Who Takes a Job in the Same Building as Her Ex-Husband?

It's the money. The building — seven stories tall, dark green, attached parking garage, the man-made lake surrounded by orange and dying trees in the fall, where one can walk during lunch hour, where we'd take the stroller on weekends. Once, before all of it, with just our son, we heard a woman screaming as if attacked in her large, gray fortress-like house. You, being the volunteer fireman you are, called out, "Is everything okay?" You inched off the sidewalk, onto the grassy hill, looking up. The windows and doors were all open, the pool empty of water, the echoes bounced off nothing but walls. She called out something — vehemently demanding us to go away. What did she have to scream about in her castle? I said someday we'd build a house like that. You agreed. We figured she was yelling at a servant. People never appreciate what they have.

You wanted to leave. It was a Sunday morning a year later. You ran down the stairs, got in your car. Somehow, pregnant, I chased. I stood in front of your car as you slowly inched out of the garage. I shook my head. Our son, only two and a half, was upstairs watching TV. I held my belly. You held my stare. You honked. I wondered if the neighbors were watching from their windows, calling the police. You gunned the motor. I stepped out of the way. I didn't care if you ran me over — my life was over, but my baby — I let you go. Back inside, I paced, wondering if you were going to her, wondering if you would come back, wondering if you'd kill yourself, you had said something about it once. I grabbed our son, strapped him in the car seat and off we went. I drove past the woman's house down in the bad part of town. A small, two-bedroom house built in the 40's or 50's. Her car wasn't there and neither was yours. I drove past the firehouse. Your car wasn't there. I drove to the parking garage of your office building. Just weeks ago you told a story of how a man had offed himself in his car on the 4th level of the parking garage. Everyone in the company was still shocked; counselors were brought in to talk to those disturbed by the incident. I drove around and around. I was nauseous from the baby, from the whirling of pillars as I went up and up in the garage. No cars. I wondered if there were security cameras. I wondered if anyone was watching on weekends. I got to the top level — the sunlight shone on your car parked there. And my imagination saw you slumped in your seat, dead, or on the pavement, stories below, flung yourself over the side. As I parked next to your car, I looked over scared to see if you were there. Scared if you weren't there. I bumped my car against the cement half-wall. I slammed the truck into park. My hands were shaking. I peeked over. You weren't there. I told our son, "Mommy will be right back." And I got out. Made sure the keys were in my hand. I went to the edge and looked down. No dead man. Furious you hadn't done away with yourself here or there, I called your work number. I left a message. *I'm here. I'm next to your car. We need to talk I have our son.*

Maybe it sounded like a threat. I guess it did. You returned the call. Said you'd meet me by the front doors and we sat in the lobby. I was coaxing you to return. You, in sweatpants, unshaven, running your hands through your unwashed hair. And even as I said whatever it was, I didn't want you to come back. I wanted this to be done. I told you I had driven by her house. You said you'd never go to her again. You didn't want her. You wanted me, our son, our baby. I wanted you to come home and victory was you, defeated, going to your car with us, but once home, I was sad I had brought you back.

Now two years later, our kids are in daycare every weekday, we're divorced and I work in the same building as you. The only job I could find and every day I see your mistress. In the bathroom. In the hall. You two walking out to lunch. I just smile. I took this job for the money, but on my lunch breaks I walk around that lake, that man-made lake, and watch the geese, the leaves dance in the wind, and wonder how a man can leave his children, his wife and then I count my steps back to my desk.

Cat, 30
Nebraska

More to Lose

I was reading a bedtime story to my two-year-old daughter when I felt a pinching cramp. When I saw the deep red bloom against the white bowl of the toilet, I knew. You'd think that having a child waiting for her mommy to come back and read the rest of her bedtime story would make it easier, but it didn't.

It was harder the second time.

The first time, it was early. I'd been to the doctor for the physical exam to verify I was pregnant as soon as the home pregnancy test was positive, but hadn't yet seen the fuzzy outline of our embryo on an ultrasound screen. When I started bleeding, I didn't know if it was a miscarriage or not. Even when the ultrasound tech asked about my dates and the ER doctor said "not all bleeding means a miscarriage," my husband and I held on to the hope that it wasn't happening to us.

When it became clear that it was a miscarriage, my best friend was there with tea and soup and chocolate and her arms wrapped tight around me while I had contractions on my couch, tears in both our eyes. The embryo had ceased to be at five weeks, I was about eight weeks when the bleeding began. My os, the opening to my cervix, didn't open, so I had a D&C to remove the products of conception.

We grieved and waited patiently until we could try again — I didn't have a normal cycle until the month the first baby would have been due. And that month, that first regular cycle, we got pregnant again. I was nervous the whole first trimester, but each time we went to the doctor, there was a strong heartbeat and a fuzzy image on the ultrasound screen. And I felt terribly sick, the worse the nausea, the heaviness, the tiredness, the more reassured I was. I carried full term and delivered a baby girl.

The second time, it was harder.

I'd already seen the fuzzy outline of our little bean on the ultrasound, its heart fluttering at 158 beats per minute. I'd had one healthy child, so I didn't expect another miscarriage. That best friend, who was there when I lost the first one, was now dead. I felt the accumulation of so much loss — the loss of the first baby, the loss of my best friend, and now the loss of the second baby. And let's face it, one miscarriage could be a fluke, two is a failure. My body was failing me, failing to create and hold on to life.

The loss was keener this time. That first miscarriage occurred when all my body understood of the pregnant condition was that ball of rapidly dividing cells fluttering through my uterus, and not the tiny human baby that smells like breast milk and new skin, that fits perfectly into the crook of my arm, that fills my heart with more love than I ever felt possible. The experience of motherhood made me understand the depth of that second loss: not cells, a child.

That second time, when I was nearing the end of the first trimester and the nausea suddenly stopped, I wasn't tired and my breasts didn't hurt, suspicion flitted through my mind. When sudden cramping led to tell-tale blood, I knew to expect a loss. I didn't hold onto hope when the ultrasound tech asked about my dates or when the ER doctor said bleeding doesn't always mean miscarriage. I knew better.

I sat quietly while I waited for all the tests to confirm what I already knew — If I was honest — what I had known the previous week when I'd suddenly felt no longer pregnant: there was no more fluttering heartbeat inside me. The baby had died. I lay in bed that night with my husband and we cried. Over the next few days, I'd cry a few more times. Privately, I'd let the tears fall when I was alone in the bathroom with all that blood.

Since the bleeding began over the weekend, I went to see the on-call Ob-Gyn at my clinic on Monday. I hadn't passed the tissue yet so at his recommendation, we scheduled a D&C.

That night, I had contractions constantly for five hours. I tried to sleep but couldn't. I lay on the couch with a heating pad over my abdomen watching Drew Barrymore and Hugh Grant flirt in *Music & Lyrics*, and willing my pain away. My daughter woke up at 2am calling for me. I went upstairs and lay with her until she fell back asleep and then went to the bathroom and with one large cramp, felt something slip out. I recognized that feeling — it was the release of birth.

The toilet was so dark with blood, I couldn't see anything. The contractions stopped. I fought back my tears and went to sleep. The next day, my Ob-Gyn did an ultrasound before the D&C and confirmed that I passed the products of conception during the night. She cleared out the remaining tissue so I could start anew.

There was no more physical pain, but I spotted for a long time. And my hormone levels didn't return to normal in the usual two weeks — my HCG was still elevated, which required me to go into the doctor's office for blood tests to make sure the levels were declining. Each positive pregnancy test and trip to the doctor's office for a blood test drew out the loss. And there was the weight. Seven pounds of swollen abdomen and thighs, enough to make none of my pants fit. The irony of wearing elastic maternity bands and positive pregnancy tests with no baby inside felt like a cruel joke.

I put the ultrasounds and sympathy cards away in a drawer. I explained to my two-year-old that the baby went away. I felt sad and alone and discouraged. I reached out to family and friends, more so than I did the first time. I even went public on facebook in an effort to take a stand so that other women wouldn't have to feel as alone as I felt. But it wasn't enough.

I went to the nursery and meticulous combed through row after row of flowering plants. It was such a hard decision, trying to choose plants for my garden to symbolize my lost children. Each time I knelt down to examine a bloom or the tag, my throat tightened and I had to breathe deep to keep from crying. I needed something that would thrive in part sun, that would grow year after year, that would be joyful and beautiful and bright. Everything my missing children would've been.

I brought home a bright orange tiki torch coneflower for the first and a raspberry wine bee balm for the second. I carefully dug the appropriate sized holes, spread their roots and planted them next to each other near the center of my garden. They bloom at different times during the summer and every time I look at them, I feel peaceful. It is as if the living energy of the children hasn't been completely lost.

Now my HCG is normal, the weight is gone and I've even had a couple of regular menstrual cycles. And although we still want another child, we're not trying.

Yet.

> "Help Inspire Others is an important project that fills a great need in our society. Miscarriage and other struggles with pregnancy are not often talked about, even among family or friends, which can lead to feelings of isolation. Help Inspire Others provides a space for these stories to be shared, providing healing for both the writers and any individuals seeking comfort while experiencing their own private struggles. It is a way to connect with others and inspire hope, and you can't put a value on that."

Melissa Doffing, 31
Minnesota

Below Zero

A dimness has poured over the bright of her day,
where dirty light tightens around the body,
squeezing bitter truth from lemon flavored karma.

An infant's voice bounces and plays inside her head,
where love is a pale, frozen rainbow; shining
just faintly above an empty playground.

The choice came with the crystal air of a cruel winter.
The day was cold — unforgivably cold — but heat
danced though it,
No one would come close to understanding this.

Now, she is rigid; severely pensive beneath falling white.
Acrobatic thoughts dissolve within her stillness as winter
coils around her, ready to strike:

And in the icy wind, a baby cries.
Tiny footprints in the snow fade away.
Where once was a life is now empty space—
empty space with a fading lullaby.

Jason Sturner
Tennessee

Miracles

I am the mother of a child neither I nor the world has ever seen. Many years ago, during her eleventh week of life, I wrote her out of my own life by choosing to have an abortion.

Not many of those years have passed without thought of her, and, two children later, she remains my first child. Most of my life has been spent either pushing the memories away or trying to make my life add up to something worthy of those eleven weeks.

Perhaps this is the reason God sent me into teaching high school kids. The principal would say I teach Language Arts, but I would hope I teach more than that. I would hope I teach love, tolerance, and respect. The latter, to me, are far more important than the former. Up until now, I would have said that I had been through high school once and learned what I was supposed to learn. I am a teacher, after all, not a student.

Then I met Amy — a ninth-grader who despised me even more than she despised English, and if you know anything about high school kids, you can imagine how much animosity that adds up to. There's a reason the teachers that end up as victims in mystery books are English teachers. She hated the way I taught, the way I graded, and even the way I patiently refused to hate her back. She couldn't understand that. She was used to people — especially teachers — hating her.

She tried diligently to change my opinion of her. It started with talking when she shouldn't have. She copied published stories instead of writing her own. She whispered comments about me to other students. Time and again, I disciplined her and then acted as if she'd done nothing worthy of anger. Finally, she publicly accused me of altering her grades based on my dislike for her.

The principal promptly assigned her two weeks of in-house suspension, which is really tough for the kids to take. Work is the only release from boredom, and the students hate to work all day. Two weeks of work seemed insufferable to Amy, and she begged me to change the punishment to something else. Anything else.

We made a deal. For a month, she would lose half of her lunch time to stay in my room and work on the assignments I gave her. If her attitude resumed its prior course, she would go to in-house. At any time, I could send her to in-house.

I didn't know if she'd be able to change because she resented me so much. Yet, day by day, I watched her become a quiet and respectful student, showing me a side of her I couldn't have imagined. We began to explore mutual respect, and even as things settled into a pleasant routine, both of our lives were about to change. About a week after our confrontation, she found out she was pregnant. Hours later, the whole school knew.

At times, I wondered if, in my hurry to end her behavior problems, I had failed her by not realizing the true cause of her frustration. How long had she feared being pregnant before that fear had been confirmed? Often I wished I could tell her something to ease her pain. I wished I could tell her that she was not alone and that I had been in her place once, and that I had chosen the "easier" and less humiliating choice.

Weeks went by and I watched Amy back away from her peers, guarding herself against the cruelty of both students and teachers who never considered how much courage it must have taken for that fifteen year-old to let the world know she had made a mistake. How many of those girls who were laughing at her had been pregnant and taken the same route as I had? Was that what society truly thought better? Was she so much worse because she hadn't made the second mistake?

For the rest of the school year, we developed a quiet trust, and all that summer I worried about her, knowing how slim the chances were that she would return to school. A week into the first term she still hadn't shown up. I was frantic. Then one day she appeared in my doorway and said, in her soft voice, "Hello."

I know my face must have glowed as I simply said, "I am so glad to see you. I've really missed you." Tears pricked my eyes and I blinked them away.

She looked doubtful, incredulous, amazed. But it was true. I had missed her. All summer I thought about the parallels between my situation at fourteen and hers at fifteen. I also thought about the differences. Twice she had taught me the meaning of courage. The first time came when she approached me and asked for a gentler punishment than in-house. How much nerve had it taken to ask someone she truly thought hated her for a kindness she really didn't expect to be given? Then secondly when she made the choice to keep the baby — a choice I had not been brave enough to make. She had let everyone in the world see just how remarkable she was, but even so, some people mocked her. Others degraded her. Still, those who really know the price she had paid believed in her.

Not long after she returned to school, she asked me to be her homebound teacher. Again, she asked me for kindness, and I felt blessed. She could've chosen any other teacher, and yet she picked me, the one she believed so strongly to have hated her. I visited her three times a week, and we often joked about the year before when she almost failed my class. She said she was planning to go to college, and was thinking about becoming a Spanish/English teacher or maybe even a doctor.

When she worked on her assignments, she sometimes called herself stupid and I corrected her. That is the only thing she ever said to me that I refused to hear. After all, she has one of the wisest hearts I've ever known, and if the heart is wise, how can the rest be any less? She wanted to go to college. I wanted that for her more than anything.

After Amy had given birth, I visited her in the hospital and she asked me to hold her son, a miracle named Anthony. For a moment, I simply stared at her baby and ached over the choice I had made, a choice I knew I could never change. I picked him up and felt the warmth of his innocent beauty rush through me. I stared at his thick black hair and long eyelashes. I placed my finger in his palm and he gripped it tightly, just as his mother had held onto him even in his first months of life. And then he yawned. Amy and I both laughed, and, at that moment, I wished I could have told her how strong she truly was and how greatly I admired her for all she was and all she would become.

I once believed my choice was a mistake, but Amy taught me that it's only a mistake if I refuse to learn from it. And I have learned many times over the years. I had thought I had learned all I needed to know, but I realized that as teachers, we come to our students with bruises and cuts life has drawn upon our hearts. We expect God to heal us in a way that is similar to the way we have been wounded, but sometimes the only way to heal ourselves is to heal another person. Amy was the first child I had the chance to help and nurture during what, for a while, seemed such a dark time. Thankfully, she will not be the last.

I used to wonder what name would've suited the little girl I still miss. Now I know. Amy will never know just how much hope she gave the teacher she thought hated her.

Some miracles just take longer than others.

> "As someone who believes the only good which can come out of mistakes, I've written a novel *October Breezes*, as a way to help other women deal with the effects of abortion."

Maria Rachel Hooley, 42
Oklahoma

Congratulations?

I remember it like it was yesterday…isn't that what everyone usually says? The day I found out I was pregnant was one of the most intense, emotional days I have ever experienced. I went to the doctor after taking eight pregnancy tests. After I saw the faint blue line that completed the small plus sign, I pulled another test out and took another one. After the third one, I thought, maybe it was wrong. I went downstairs and started drinking all sorts of things…like milk, orange juice, and a ton of water like that would change the already telling plus sign into a minus sign?

The next morning I called the doctor's office. The receptionist answered the phone. I explained to her that I thought I was pregnant. I guess…by the sound of my voice, she could tell I was young and she asked…

"Are you keeping it?"

"Really?" I thought to myself… "Did she just ask me that?" I was taken back…"I think so…I'm not sure…" I said I wasn't sure even though I was sure I was keeping this baby. I called my friend Suzanne, and asked her to go with me to my appointment, which was that day.

As we pulled up to the doctor's office, I could feel my heart's heavy beat in my throat. I lit up a cigarette and made a conscience decision that this may very well be my last cigarette for the next nine months. If I wasn't pregnant, I decided I would come out and finish off the brand new pack. I mean could all of those eight pregnancy tests I took the day before have false results? I never thought I'd be faced with this situation. I was 20 years old about to turn 21 — finishing college…just about to feel real freedom and this is what I was doing, sitting in a car with Suzanne waiting to find out if my life would forever change. The actual time spent in the doctor's office really feels like a blur to me. I felt like time couldn't move fast enough…After I took the ninth pregnancy test at the doctor's, I sat in his office with Suzanne waiting to hear the results. My feet, clad in Converse, twitched.

"Well," the doctor began to say..."your pregnancy test was positive." I felt my whole body sink into the chair...I felt the room closing in around me, and before I could breathe out — he finished with this..."But we can't see the sac." What does this mean...I thought...my mouth was dry and a million thoughts rushed past me, as if there was some escape...He explained to me and Suzanne that there was a possibility that I could have an ectopic pregnancy...and that I'd have to come in for the rest of the week for blood tests and sonograms until they saw the baby in the uterus. Could it be fatal? Yes. It didn't actually hit me until later that night how serious this situation could be. Suzanne asked a few questions for me, as I sat next to her in such shock that I couldn't even speak. As we left the doctor's office, he looked at me with a half smile and said...

"Congratulations?"

I just quietly said, "Thanks."

We walked out into the hallway, and it wasn't until the door closed behind us that I broke down...and she broke down for me. I cried and cried and cried. I could barely remember what just took place just minutes before we ended up in the hallway crying. I was scared, terrified...I felt so blank — so empty. My stomach hurt from crying so hard. I felt sick. After crying for a long time, I could finally begin to hear some of my own thoughts. The only one what was the most evident was *what were my parents going to think? How am I going to tell my parents?* We made our way out to the car where we just sat. Not only was I pregnant — but there was a chance of an ectopic pregnancy. So not only did I have to sit in a room with my parents and tell them I was single and pregnant with a boy they never met or heard of BUT ALSO I had to tell them there was a chance the baby was developing in the wrong place.

How am I going to do this?

Melissa Ferina, 24
New York

Just Like Me

Despite several empathetic attempts at focusing my attention on the newspaper in front of me, I cannot help overhearing the women in the next booth. By the time my meal arrives, I am disturbingly interested in their conversation, until they start talking about their kids. The more I try to ignore them, the harder it is to tear my attention away, like driving by the scene of an accident. One of the women is talking about her son who is about to become a teenager.

"My baby's growing up so fast," she says softly, her voice beginning to shake. My stomach tightens with jealousy. Some babies don't get to grow up.

I watch my daughter walk into the Kindergarten room at Hilltop Elementary School, marveling at her confidence. The other kids walk in with the usual first-day uncertainty, each step timid and small. Jasmine, on the other hand, walks with purpose, heading straight for the coat racks where she immediately finds her name. We worked on her letters and numbers over the summer and Jasmine picked up the concepts easily. I was determined to arm my daughter with as many tools as possible before sending her into the world of academia.

Jasmine carefully hangs up her pink "Dora the Explorer" backpack, the one that took two hours and three stores to find. It matches her shoes, which in turn matches her shirt. I would normally prefer to lead Jasmine away from the materialistic pressures of society, but the first day of school is different. We spent an entire Saturday shopping and laughing, preparing for this moment. She smiles as she hangs up her pack and turns to face the room, subtle blond curls bouncing off her shoulders. She finds her desk and proudly sits down, poised and ready to begin her education. I try to imagine what she is thinking.

I began imagining Jasmine the moment I found out I was pregnant. Would she share my love of books? Like to cuddle? Be afraid of the dark? I pictured my mother and me, standing in the kitchen of my childhood home two hours past curfew, and the venom in her eyes as she hoped I would have a child "just like me."

Now that I was an adult, I wondered if my mother would look upon her grandchild with pride, grateful that she was "just like me." I tried to imagine what Jasmine would dream about, who she would become. Of course, the only thing that mattered was having a happy and healthy baby, but secretly I believed that my child was going to change the world.

Jasmine didn't start Kindergarten this year, although she would have. I share that milestone with every other parent, although I don't have pictures to post on Facebook or send to the grandparents. She won't trick-or-treat in October either, but I will see her every time I open the door to a princess with blond hair and blue eyes. There will never be a sixth birthday party, but that doesn't mean Jasmine will never turn six. Time has never stopped. I only carried Jasmine for a few months, but I never lost her.

Jamee Larson, 38
Minnesota

The Starting Line

I was in trouble. The kind that my mother had harangued her six daughters against in all my memories, the biggest trouble there was in a family of eleven short of jail. The year was 1983, the month November. I was sixteen, the youngest of nine, my mother's last hope that she had parented correctly, the nonsmoking non beer drinking straight A student, proof of her parental skill, proof that she wasn't to blame for the others turning out bad. There had been the sexual molestation episode by a family friend back in 79, but she'd buried that in her brain somewhere amongst the other unmentionable family secrets. Don't talk about it and it never happened.

When children turn out bad, my mother yelled with each whack of the broom on my sisters' shoulders, they make the parents look bad, too. Although I thought she was demon-like, spit flying with the force of her words and the power of her broom, I see with the wisdom of the years packed tight in my brain, that she was right about children's behavior reflecting on the parents. When my own daughter, Morgan, goes outside barefoot and jacketless in the Maine spring weather, I know the neighbors are judging me. If I happen to see the man who lives next door, I run outside, a size seven parker in my hands as evidence, and explain how my daughter has lots of sweaters and shoes but refuses to wear them. I never got hit with the broom, only the yardstick, sometimes a spoon. The broom was reserved for the smokers and the drinkers, and those who played loose with keeping their clothes on in front of boys. I tried hard to hold onto my goodness and my clothes, but when I met Eric my behavior no longer seemed like something I could control. I was desperate to be with him. I lost my ability to reason, to think, to care what anyone else thought. I risked trouble without believing that anything like trouble could befall me. This new person in my life made me feel safe, protected, and loved in a way I didn't know was possible. Trouble happened to other people. I'd witnessed it many times, the fights and the punishments. Not me, I'd thought. I understood the meaning behind the warning

"Don't get too carried away." I had witnessed two sisters pregnant before high school graduation, so I knew better.

It's odd how we think we know things without having experienced them. And it's odd how a person can be in so much trouble on the inside but no one can see it on the outside, all the evidence hidden, working beneath the radar. In the beginning of my trouble, there were times I thought I'd averted it and would run to the bathroom to check. But with a renewed sense of doom wriggling its aggressive tentacles in my gut, I'd leave the bathroom, trembling in anticipation of what I knew I couldn't escape. Usually, I loathed the feel of anything sliding forth and sullying my underpants. My mother wouldn't allow any of her girls to wear tampons because they simulated intercourse, and she didn't need her daughters getting any ideas, so we wore thick generic pads that sat stiff between our legs, the bulky outlines evident to any eyes that glanced across our bottoms. We were all on a one pad per day allotment. Combined with one shower a week regimen, the reality of menstruation was formidable. Dreaded until the reason for its nonappearance hit you with a power that reverberated to a tingling sensation in your head that indicated an approaching panic attack. I wandered through my classes at school with all my attention focused on sensing a cramp, a discharge of fluid. Hope would flare and die. And no one shared those few weeks of silent agony with me except for my partner in crime, the boy I planned to marry, the boy who asked each time I saw him, "Did you start yet?" This question, a consistent reminder of my failure to succeed in the twenty-eight day cycle, caused me to burst forth with fury. "Don't you think I'd tell you if I did?"

Five days late, ten, fifteen, and still I didn't start. Start can mean so many things: a new project, a book, classes, homework, dinner. But here start meant only my deficiency to menstruate, a simple biological event that other girls succeeded at all over the world with the exceptions of gymnasts and super models, with the exception of bad girls.

"This doesn't mean you're bad," Eric whispered as he hugged me. "You're good and we're in this together." This after the genetic witch voice within my brain had attacked him.

I wanted to believe him, but nausea bit at a foreign emptiness in my stomach and fatigue embedded itself into the fibers of my muscles. When I looked up at his smiling face with those chimpanzee-like eyes, I knew that "in this together" meant something completely different for him. His clothes wouldn't get tighter, he could walk past any adult and not turn heads, make people think of sex. I couldn't keep my eyes open in geometry. He could and he did. The teacher spoke nonsense. My brain decided it was too much work to figure out the angles, the proofs. This was not information I needed anymore. Balking, turning inward, my brain told me I needed to eat a hamburger. I'm a vegetarian so I vomited.

"You're going to be okay," Eric said. "You'll see." He wiped my face, placing the strands of throw-up dampened hair away from my mouth. I couldn't see what he saw. I was too tired, exhausted from feeling everyone's silent criticism. Teachers judged me with their non-smiles and unpleasant tones. I assumed all humans thought I was one of those bad girls, a stupid girl. I wanted nothing more than for people to think that I was intelligent and good, like they used to. I returned from school to my dog Joplin who treated me like a hero because I could open the refrigerator. I wanted to live forever with dogs, just dogs.

Desperate to eat I opened the fridge a lot. "Why are you frying all those potatoes?" my mother pointed accusingly at the cast iron pan. "Why are you eating so much?" she stared at my stomach, my breasts. Could she see that they ached? Guilt charged through my middle. Her voice got harder and her eyes got smaller, "What's going on?" I couldn't answer her. If I didn't eat the potatoes, I would throw up. I couldn't get them in fast enough. They didn't seem to touch the empty recess that was my stomach. So much effort to fill it, then one slice of potato too many. How would I ever learn the fine line between starving and overeating? I threw up noticing with fascination how little I'd chewed any of them, one more heave, all of them.

"Are you pregnant?" my mother demanded. Not, Are you sick? Or even a polite, what's wrong? She assumed that I'd turned bad based on a pan of wasted fried potatoes, possibly because waste of any type sent her flying off the handle. My sister, one of the ones who had sex as a teenager but didn't get pregnant, explained that flying off the handle meant a witch got so angry she fell off her broom. My mother assessed me like she would a pound of ground meat that was the right color but smelled the wrong way. Years of my good behavior erased in the second it takes sperm to escape a pinhole in a condom. If not for that hole, that one percent risk, there would be no trouble, and I'd still be considered good.

"I don't know," I said, opening a can of baked beans.

"How did this happen?" her voice and face fierce.

"I don't know." I didn't point out that she, mother of nine, should know this detail. My knowledge on the subject was shaky. What little I knew was the result of someone in the school administration thinking reproduction should be taught as part of the curriculum.

"You don't know?" she yelled in disbelief, the volume escalating, "How can you not know? How could you do this to us?"

I took my beans out of the microwave and settled in for the tirade of how I was ruining her and my father's lives. She should know from the evidence of my condition that I was not the one with the answers.

"You're no different from your sisters," she continued on, her tone matching the wheeking of a guinea pig desperate for celery. "Didn't you learn anything from watching all their mistakes?" I didn't defend myself. I didn't tell her I wanted to be different. I didn't tell her that pregnancy took two people and she was laying all the blame on me. "You're not alone," Eric had said, but he wasn't the one sitting here with canned beans getting yelled at. I was the one who would be judged by appearance alone in the months to come. Yes, I had learned from watching. I'd used protection, and I didn't think it would happen to me.

"What's your father going to say to this?" my mother broke into my self-pity, my sudden and overwhelming fatigue. It would take a huge effort for me to wash my bowl in the sink.

"I'm sorry," I said. And I really was, when seconds later I kneeled on the bathroom floor and threw up all the pinto beans, knowing I was going to have to start all over again to fill the emptiness.

Days passed and my father said nothing. He didn't look me in the eye. I was invisible. My mother took me to the gynecologist, taking me out of school for the November 16th appointment. It felt wrong, almost painful, not to be in class with everyone else, with Eric. A schoolgirl version of a vampire, I wasn't supposed to be out in the day. The office nurse weighed me in at 116 pounds. She took my blood pressure. I peed in a cup and seconds later I put on a paper gown. The doctor knocked gently and entered.

Him: "How are you today?"

Me: Silent, what could I say? Should I show regret at my condition? Proper mortification?

Him: "I need to ask a few questions before we get started."

Me: Silent, but nodding, my mother to the side of me. I am locked in embarrassment and fear that he will ask something that will get me in even more trouble later. Can I lie? Is this like the witness stand?

Him: "Date of last menstrual period?"

Me: "September 28th."

Him: "Do you smoke?"

Me: "No." But if I did would I admit it in front of my mother?

Him: "Do you drink?"

Me: "No." But again, if I did?

Him: He laughs. "You're the first pregnant teenager in here who has no bad habits."

Me: I laugh awkwardly. I know he's trying to break the tension. He can see how difficult this is with my mother fuming with whatever emotions she's experiencing to the right of me.

Him: "Do you know who the father is?"

Me: I am fiercely offended. Is this a roundabout way of calling me a slut? I know I look shocked because I can feel that my mouth is open. "Yes."

Him: "And that would be?"

Me: "Eric Peppe." I see him write the name down on his clipboard. Even if I don't marry Eric, my medical record will always read, "Eric Peppe, father of baby."

Him: Short silence, then surprise, "Oh, Eric, I know him. He teaches my daughter piano. Talented young man."

Me: I smile carefully. How do I respond? With pleasure at the connection? Can I be pleased? Should I be worried? Will he remove his daughter from lessons, from Eric's bad influence? What are the rules of this doctor patient relationship and my teenage pregnancy status? I don't know the protocol, and I wish there was a book I could read to discover the answers.

The doctor told me to lie back. He smiled and asked me to scoot my bottom toward him legs spread wide with my feet in stirrups. My first pelvic exam was everything I'd been taught never to do in front of a male. Hot blood pulsed in my face. Blood, the life force, my uterus withheld for another life. Without blood coursing through the veins and arteries there can be no intercourse. There can be no pregnancy. Blood flows hot and then blood is stored within. There could be another reason for a missed period or unpredictable vomiting. Lots of people throw up and aren't pregnant. The doctor, a gynecologist or in my case obstetrician, made the pregnancy real and with that confirmation, my mother's anger escalated as if even she hadn't believed I was pregnant until someone with a speculum and white coat said the words.

Each day post the doctor visit, I returned from school to face my mother's disappointment at the door. Our conversations were careful: nothing about pregnancy, babies, my relationship with Eric, or my discomfort. I was too embarrassed, too busy trying not to throw up the last thing I ate to speak at all. I wore my fear of being found out at school like a cloak. In September I'd been chosen by the guidance counselor to be one of the two peer facilitators in my high school. I spent one period a day explaining the college application process to freshman. I had been on the college track myself and now I didn't know what my future held. My plan had been to marry Eric, move to Portland, and go to school full-time. Would a baby change that? There were too many unknowns, all scary in their lack of solidity that I concentrated only on the hour ahead of me, tried not to see into the future that parental adults told me I'd destroyed.

No one told Eric that he had ruined his future. He was a pianist, amazingly talented, people said, winner of competitions, gifted and smart. Except for the scrawl of his name on my chart, he was still all of those things. His career was not, as my mother said about mine, "down the toilet. I'd thrown everything down the toilet."

Eric chose to tell his divorced father when we went out for ice cream. He announced it at the Auburn Goodwins, and I wondered if anyone else recognized the irony of good and wins blinking in neon across our booth table. His father's eyes widened at the news, opening wider with disbelief and a dash of horror.

"Well, what are you going to do now?" he said, thinking like my mother, that I had all the answers.

"Whatever we need to," Eric said and I was grateful for the "we."

"What do you mean we? This is her problem and she needs more than you to help her." He looked at me because I was the pregnant party.

"You know what this means don't you?"

I was only sixteen how could I know much of anything? "What?" I said, ready to hear, ready for some solution.

"You have a decision to make. There's abortion and adoption to consider."

I shook my head. "I could never do that."

He stared at me without drinking his coffee. My mouth dared me to take another bite of my hot fudge sundae. I touched the spoon and my stomach decided that was far enough. If you even look at it, my stomach told my brain, you will throw up. Eric could see the forces taking sides, gaining strength. I swallowed, clamped my teeth together, averted my eyes. He covered the ice cream with a napkin and pushed it to the opposite side of the table. In that moment, I knew I would love him forever.

The next day, Eric's mother accepted the news as if she knew it'd been inevitable. She didn't make any suggestions or ask any questions. Instead she invited me to Thanksgiving. No one mentioned the pregnancy. It was all I could think about, always there at the front of my mouth. I'm pregnant, I thought when I woke up. I'm pregnant, I thought when I went to sleep.

My stomach swelled, but not noticeably to outsiders. It could have been all the potatoes I ate, sitting in there in one great lump. I woke up one morning and didn't vomit, but I had an ache in my right side. Early December, the time when teenagers are thinking ahead to Christmas, I told my mother about the persistent pain. This day, December 5th, maybe because of midterms, maybe because of the holiday season, I went to the gynecologist after school and Eric insisted on coming, too. The nurse weighed me. I'd gained four pounds. The doctor ordered an ultrasound. There was a fetal sac but no heartbeat. His patience and kindness unsettled me and irritated my mother. No one should treat me nicely. I had done a bad thing.

"It's still early," the doctor said. "Too early to know anything for sure. Everything else is within normal limits."

First I was late and now I was early. "But the ache," I asked. I usually didn't speak. I let other people talk for me. I knew I looked stupid, pregnant at sixteen. I didn't want to sound the part, too.

"The ovary looks normal. It's likely gas pain," he said. "Pregnant women experience a lot of gas." He sent me home and said to come back for a second ultrasound in two weeks.

Pregnant women. I was pregnant but hadn't yet thought of myself as a woman. I was having difficulty adjusting to my new identity, one that included vomit, weight gain, and gas. I wondered if pregnant women were past the age of sticking their thumbs on their foreheads to falsely signal their passing gas innocence.

Time slowed to a trickle. I'd been eager many years for independence and a home of my own, usually one that included unlimited chocolate and dogs, but since I'd met Eric two years previously I had a solid plan. When I turned eighteen, we'd get married and move to another town, maybe another state. I'd been crossing the days off my calendar for two years and I had two more years to go, halfway there, but these last pregnancy weeks had seemed the slowest of my life. First the uncertainty, the waiting to know if I was pregnant, and now the waiting for a second ultrasound to see if there was a fetus. Watching the clock, watching the calendar days, wishing my life away second by second because time seemed endless.

I don't have to struggle to remember the feeling of imprisonment. Time had me on all sides. I look back at that younger self and I worry she doesn't know what she was doing, wishing her life away like that. I know if she'd had a magic lamp, she would have asked that genie to add four years to her life the day she saw Eric playing Randy Newman's "Short People" in chorus and thought, "I'm going to marry that piano playing boy." I know that before she met Eric, she would have asked the genie to add any number of years to get her grown and out. She might have missed meeting him then. The present self thinks the lack of a genie appearing before ninth grade was probably in her best interests, but the torture of waiting those last four years probably took twice as many years off her life and his.

The two weeks did pass because they always do. December 20th arrived and many people were feeling festive and generous. When I lay on the exam table the cold gel on my abdomen, I didn't feel excitement for Christmas or a new year. I felt nothing that I can remember except sadness when the radiologist couldn't locate a heartbeat and then the gynecologist told me there was no fetus. I had a nonviable pregnancy, a blighted ovum. The news wasn't welcome to me like it was to my mother and Eric's father. Disaster grazed but did not strike. For my mother, this eight week incident would go the way of the sexual molestation when I was twelve. We would never speak of it and if we remained silent long enough, we could pretend it never happened.

If the fetal sac wasn't removed immediately by dilatation and curettage, painful miscarriage would begin, probably over the holidays. On December 21st, I put on a hospital gown in the day surgery of Central Maine Medical Center, and the nurse led me to a semi-private room. Eric sat with me, a biography of George Gershwin beside him, and we began the wait for surgery, for someone to come and bring me to the operating room. My mother left after signing papers, but would return in a few hours. Why was I, were we both, somber? Regretful? Sad? Why, when I had feared pregnancy so much and pleaded with the pregnancy gods to make my period begin, was I sad that it was over? I didn't have the experience or the knowledge then, twenty-eight years ago, to understand, to articulate the insights that the passage of time brings. I see those two kids sitting in that hospital room and I remember how offended I was that so many had called us kids. "You're children yourselves," they'd accused. "How can you have a baby?" But being a kid is no crime, a kid in love even less so. Why then do I still feel that I have to hide this event from people, that their opinion of me will change if they find out I was a pregnant teenager? Why do I still feel guilt? Embarrassment? Why do I still feel that I was bad?

I study the memory I have of that young couple who sat on the edge of a hospital bed holding hands, and I experience again a sense of loss and regret and so does my husband. Eric says, "I wonder sometimes, what if the pregnancy had been real? Would we have three kids or would we have stopped at two and never known Morgan?" Still the unknowns, still the lack of answers.

I understand the sadness I felt that day, a sadness that wasn't acceptable for sexually active teenagers to voice out loud because we should be cheering our good luck. Even though I'd been afraid of my parents, and Eric had been nervous of his, the creation of life is exciting in all its possibility and its mystery, and there is an emotional cost when it's taken away. My present self knows what my past self also knows about the day my sentence of trouble would be lifted, the evidence removed, and I would avoid this kind of trouble for the next two years because the gynecologist, without the permission of my mother, prescribed birth control pills. Eric and I waited four days before Christmas, barely speaking, just happy to be together. Then a nurse came in, and I tried not to allow myself to think she was judging me, judging us, when she said to Eric, "You can wait for her here. We're ready to start."

Helen Peppe, 44
Maine

You Who Never Lay in My Arms

Twice I found myself unexpectedly pregnant. Twice I chose to end those pregnancies. Two hundred thousand times, I have found myself dwelling on those losses trying again to justify them. There are no support groups for women who have had abortions; there are only picket lines to cross and crosses to bear.

I have to somehow forgive myself the abortions I have endured. I have to believe that the beloveds who never lay in my arms had purpose just the same, had lives that counted no matter how short, and had teachings that were deep and meaningful. The concealment of this act is depleting and humiliating. The making of the choice itself has its own bottomless sadness and pain, but it is the silence and secrecy enveloping it that festers in one's wounds. There is no healing in this injured void.

When did life enter my beloveds and when did life leave them? I know the little soul of my second abortion left my body before the procedure, I felt it flee and I know it was a girl. I also know that she has forgiven me even if I cannot forgive myself; she has told me as much in the maroon stillness of my mind. Forty-five and well past the time and vigor to expand our already grown family, the inconsistency of early menopause caused the "safe zone" to lack regularity. Still, a part of me wanted her. Extinguishing her potential was wretched, heartrending, yet her calling was not to tread this earth, but instead was to visit my body and mind for the briefest of moments and to clarify my future. Her spirit still comes to me when the world is muted and paused.

With my first beloved, there was a disconnect. Over a quarter century ago, a life brewed in my belly, unplanned. I was in a relationship of love and turmoil. I did not know if this partner was the "forever one" I sought, and I could not envision single parenthood. I took that beloved away from both of us with anger and uncertainty in my heart, causing no connection, no knowing of that spirit. It was a procedure of incomprehensible emptiness that left me weeping in a shrouded room with no frame of reference. I was young and alone and I stayed that way.

It's the silence; it's the way women don't share these experiences that is excruciating. With all other things, so many other things, our sharing spills like spring water from old tin buckets on hot summer days. But this sharing of abortion stories seeps, crawls, creeps and hides in cracked crevices avoiding daylight. This sharing goes unshared, and it rots the bowels of good people.

If there were a support group, what would it look like? Would it be just women? Would it meet openly or in private obscurity? In my imagined world of mercy I can envision meetings held on clear, bright days in rooms with windows, large from floor to ceiling and candles, hundreds of candles, some lit and others still waiting for their flame. We could either hold hands or simply nod. There wouldn't need to be words, just recognition and acknowledgement of impossible decisions made in despair and ultimately alone.

I can see a long line of us waiting silently to enter that sanctified room; the line would have to be long because if it were not, it would be unbearable. To be one of only a few would substantiate shame. The procession would move slowly, but as the wait had already been eternal, the painstaking, honey dripping pace would be disregarded, each woman honored with however much time she needed. One by one, we would enter this space of radiance and redemption and light a candle. Some of us would weep, others softly moan, many would just remain silent, their relief not yet revealed. Yet this small step, taken in the company of sisters who had made the same decision, done the same thing, would at last be enough.

> "Most importantly what has happened to me since exhuming this piece from its dark corner in my mind is the beginning of subtle relief I've been experiencing with the expulsion of this secret.
>
> Also, at a moment that made sense, I shared my story with my twenty one year old daughter with the hope that if she were ever faced with this most difficult of decisions, she would know she was not alone in her struggle toward a choice complicated and layered."

Nancy, 52; Massachusetts

The Broken Crystal Ball and the Zombie Killer

I was a much better parent before the birth of my son. As a single woman, I would walk through city streets, shop in local stores, stroll through the culture consuming corporation of Target eyeing the red bull's-eye of affordable ads only to be inconsiderately interrupted by the piercing wail of an unruly child. The crystal ball in my head would think when I have a child he will never behave this way. Later on that day, I would sigh loudly at a parent who thought it was acceptable to bring their whiny kid to a movie and allow *it* to *cry* loudly during the best part of my afternoon matinee. A rubbing of the crystal ball and I would see me and my immensely supportive husband guarding our child from any rated R sentiments, staying home on a Friday night enjoying family friendly carpet picnics and Disney inspired fun.

Someone shattered my crystal ball or maybe it was broken all along. Yep, I was given a defective crystal ball and if I could now get through Target without my three year old throwing a titanic-sized tantrum I would take my crystal ball back and demand a refund. Where is the supportive husband co-parenting with me like perfectly synchronized tennis doubles? Who is this kid that is taking me to task with all 39 inches of his miniature frame? Why is that woman staring at me with disgust as I carry my son kicking and screaming out of the toy aisle? As his pint sized elbows dig deeper into my side, I contemplate telling the female spectator: "Just wait and see. Your crystal ball is lying to you too." No time for daydreaming in the fulltime post of parenting. My imaginary conversation is interrupted by the warm, wet sensation of pee seeping through my shirt because colossal tantrums often result in child incontinence.

I think this all started, the broken crystal ball that is, when I was told that I was having a son. Nothing against the "snips and snails and puppy dog tales" since Mother Goose claims that's what little boys are made of, but with a series of failed relationships with men the thought of being given a "man in training" seemed like a cruel joke. I asked the doctor to check again. After all, umbilical cords can resemble super long penises on an ultra sound. The picture where my son was actually holding his unit like a prized trophy clarified that my life was indeed someone's punch line.

From one charade to the next it became mommy and son against the big bad wolf of the world. We had play dates, park trips and pediatric visits. At one doctor's appointment we were given some news no parent or child should ever have to hear. A rare condition that causes thinning in the optic nerves had compromised the vision in my son's left eye. As my own eyes began to tear up, my strong willed warrior scowled at the ophthalmologist and leaned in my direction with his arms outstretched. While bent over to hoist him from the crepe paper coated doctor's table, he took his hand and wiped away the tear descending down my cheekbone. For an encore to his dramatic display he spewed projectile vomit all over the table and floor ironically soiling everything but the protective exam table paper. At that point I knew my son's, "I'll show you attitude" would always serve him well. The question became how I would fare in his mission to prove to the doctor's, and the world, that he's the one in charge.

With a diagnosis name so long it's worthy of a Guinness Book record nod and a toy soldier toddler so willful he earned the title of Sir Joshua in all of his clinic visits, by the terrible two's, our dynamic duo became disparate arched enemies. His favorite word emerged as "No" and no amount of reverse psychology could convince my son that "No" was not an appropriate answer for all things. At one point between sleep deprivation and mental insanity I even asked him if "he wanted a million dollars?"

"NO I DON'T WANT A MILLION DOLLARS," he yelled. "NO MILLION DOLLARS MOMMY. NO MILLION DOLLARS!"

Well I want a million dollars. I deserve a million dollars. The calculated compensation of a mom should be a base salary of a million dollars.

The terrible two's extend into three's. The title is deceiving just like conjured up dreams in a crystal ball. Well beyond his third birthday "No" still remains the word of the day, only this time it's accompanied by "No I'd rather not take a nap right now." The "I'd rather" is supposed to be an example of his developmental growth in both speech and rhetoric, yet I am not impressed in the least.

Two time-outs later and he's finally asleep or so I think, until I hear a barely audible, but impassioned dialogue between my son and a zombie.

"Go to sleep, Joshua."

"I'm shooting all the zombies first."

"There are NO zombies. Sleep. Now. I'm not kidding."

"Ssh, Mommy. There the zombie is. 'Freeze, pwew pwew. You're dead.'"

My gun-slinging child pretends to blow smoke off his extended finger and curls back in the bed for a nap that should now be almost over. My anti-gun sentiments have been lost on him and the more I tell him that guns are unacceptable the more he manufactures them from legos, clothes hangers, and even the heels of my BCBG sling backs.

With his gun briefly holstered we embark on our biggest battle of the day: dinner. If it was up to him he'd eat Popsicles, soy milk and carrots, not because the carrots are vegetables and instead because he is a fan of the color orange. He's surprisingly fond of lettuce too, which makes me feel like a better-quality mom than the loud sighing, faultfinding, critical eyes of our weekly stage show at Target. Following grace and an emphatic "Amen," he likes that word just not as much as "No," the epic struggle to get tri-tip roast and vegetables down clenched teeth commences. My mind flips through my mental Rolodex of Super Nanny episodes, parenting books, and what would have happened to me if I dared refuse dinner as a child. An hour later, when we're both at the point of tears, my zombie killer asserts, "I want to be Obama."

"What did you just say?"

"I want to be Obama."

The previous evening I bargained a Popsicle with my son to turn off Barney in exchange for President Barack Obama's State of the Union Address. I endeavored to explain to him the importance of hearing what the president has to say and in my failed attempts to articulate world politics to a three year old, I eventually resorted to something about "America" and "leadership" and "because I said so." I also relented and even encouraged him to go kill zombies so mommy could listen. Instead he sat affixed to my side, clapping and cheering whenever congress applauded.

"Why do you want to be Obama, son?"

"Because I want to be the Boss of America!"

"Well to be the Boss of America you have to eat dinner."

"Who says?"

"America says. All those people clapping last night were clapping because Obama eats dinner and after dinner he oversees America."

Tri-Tip, green beans, carrots and a Popsicle all went down without a fight. Today I am a better mom than yesterday. Tomorrow I may suck, but then again my crystal ball has nothing on me and my zombie killing, soymilk drinking, boss of America, son.

Ryane Nicole, 32
California

Acknowledgments

There are so many people that have been directly and indirectly involved in the evolution of this project. Without their constant support this project would not be what it is today. There aren't words to express how much you all mean to me.

To every person who thought about submitting a story, to everyone who visited the site, and to all of you who found the courage to reach inside and share a piece of your life to reach out to others — I thank you. Without everyone who submitted their piece, this book would not exist. The amount of gratitude and respect I have for each of you is endless. What you have done for others is admirable and incredible. Thank you for your constant support, your letters, and for giving the support that others need.

Mike- Thank you for all your help with the cover and teaching me how to use paintbrush. I really appreciate it!

Danielle Degregorio- Thank you for the amazing logo, the quotes, the chats, and for being such a good friend to me.

Cathy O'Neill- Thanks for being the first person to look over my manuscript. I knew you would give me your true opinion because that is the type of person you are. I look up to you and think you are one of the strongest women I have ever known. I love you and I am so glad we met and became so close.

Stephanie Pelcher- It really amazes me how quickly two people can become so close. Thank you for your honesty, your time, and for your wonderful English skills. I am lucky to be living next door to someone like you. I am so happy you have been on this journey with me.

Claire Curry- I truly have to thank you for all your support with this. I don't think you will ever know what it meant to me that you took the time out to help me rework my introduction. You are amazing.

Danielle Rocks- You are an amazing photographer and truly a great friend. Roads may have separated us in the past but I am so glad they came together and we are the friends that we are today. I can't thank you enough for the amazing photos for the site and for the book cover. (www.daniellerocksphotography.com)

Cheryl Cruse- Thank you for listening to me constantly about the project and for motivating me to move forward. You have been such a great friend. You have been there for me through so much and I can't thank you enough.

Suzanne Smith- No matter what happens in my life I know we will always have each other. Thank you for crying with me when I found out my life would change forever. I wouldn't have wanted anyone else there besides you.

Ali Nicoletti- Thank you for being my very best friend. I cannot believe how far we have come since we were two-years-old! It is amazing how two people from such a young age can mature together into the people we are today. I appreciate you "post-it noting" the whole manuscript and giving me your honest opinion about everything. Thank you for all the long talks about this project and for constantly motivating me.

Élan- I love you. Thank you for giving out my Help Inspire Others pens at work and for being one of my biggest supporters. You have been my rock throughout this whole process and throughout my life. I am so glad we are more than sisters. I don't know where I would be without you. Thank you for believing in me and for being the sister some people wish that they had.

Craig- I am so lucky to have you to look up to and more importantly, to have you as my brother. I have always looked up to you on so many levels. All your ideas for this project have really been a huge help. Thank you for all your support — I love you more than you will ever know.

Kim- Thank you for always being there for me. I know I can always come to you with anything. Your drive and ambition has always been an inspiration to me.

My family- Each and every one of you have been nothing but supportive and encouraging throughout the past four years. I am so unbelievably lucky to have you in my life. You all have been rooting me on and keeping me going. I love you all.

The breakfast crew at The Marriott, my friends at Sanford Brown, the wonderful group of women from the Writers Conference, and Heather and Mike from my externship-Thank you for the constant support. You all have been just awesome. I am so lucky to be surrounded by such wonderful people.

My Parents- I sat across our dining room table and told you about this project. I'm sure at the time — there was no clear plan and my Dad told me to "let it take its own course." It certainly did. I will never forget how excited I was when I rented my P.O. Box. I was even more excited when I got my first piece of mail. It was a "reach for the stars" card, from my parents. My parents are the most incredible people. From the moment I told them I was having a baby until now, they have been nothing but supportive and loving. I love them with every piece of my being and without them I would be lost. I love you both so much. I am so lucky and grateful to have you — and I am honored to call you Mom and Dad.

My husband, Kevin- Wow. What a journey we have been on. I have never met someone with so much determination. There is nothing in this life that stops you from reaching for the sky. This is why I fell in love with you. I saw that determination that night in Starbucks. You are just simply an incredible man. You adopted my daughter. You gave her unconditional love and a wonderful person to look up to. I saw the way you looked at her — like you loved her and she looks at you the same way. From the day she, willingly, started calling you Daddy until now; you never cease to amaze me. I am so lucky to be motivated by you on a daily basis. Without you this project would not be what it is today. There were times I didn't know how to move forward — but you knew how and you made sure I kept going.

To my daughter, Kairi- From the moment I knew I was pregnant with you I loved you. I loved you more than I ever thought it was possible to love someone. I remember the moment I saw your beautiful face, life finally made sense. I knew my reason and my purpose. Things just became clear. My life was complete. You are the reason I started this project, and my true inspiration. You are the sun in my universe and I love you more than anything in this world. Thank you for smiling that beautiful smile everyday and for filling my heart with happiness I never knew existed.

Author's Biography

Danielle Albanese "Miracles Do Happen"
I am a single mom working at the Marriott and also working as a hairdresser. I have learned a lot about myself through my experiences and also through the people that I meet in my life day to day.

Carla "Heartbeat"
Carla is a writer and mother of two teenagers. She "brings home the oatmeal" helping others tell their stories, through her work as president/founder of iMinds PR (www.imindspr.com), and innovative advocacy, research, and outreach from Seattle to Mexico City. She is the co-founder/co-director of The Pasadena Writing Project and has been featured in a variety of publications, including The *Pasadena Weekly*, *Tikkun*, and *iVilliage*. She recently started writing a column "The Real Single Mom's of South Pasadena."
(http://southpasadena.patch.com/articles/single-moms-of-south-pas-a-flash-of-nostalgia).

Cat "Who Takes a Job in the Same Building as her Ex-husband?" Cat now teaches creative writing at the University of Nebraska, Omaha and is the marketing director of the poetry publisher, The Backwaters Press. Her work has appeared in *Sugar House Review*, *Coe Review* and other anthologies. She no longer works in the same building as her ex, thankfully. She's a single mom to two, Pierce and Leven.

Ann E. Damiano "They Weren't There (But Dedicated to Those Who Were)"
I have worked as both an administrator and faculty member in higher education for the past thirty years. My poetry has been published in *Steam Ticket 11,* a literary journal from the University of Wisconsin; *Happenings,* an alumni publication; and *Physiognomy in Letters.* I have written a memoir about growing up in suburban America in the 1960s with a brother with autism. A chapter of this memoir was published in *Siblings & Autism,* edited by Debra Cumberland and Bruce Mills. I have been married for 26 years and have two daughters.

Jan K. Dederick "A Better Night"
I am in the same house where my story happened (& where my daughter and son were born, and where I have my Health Care practice). I do

Kairos Therapy, a gentle powerful modality for emotional healing. It was what got me through my own dark night of the soul and I have helped hundreds with it. Since my kids fledged, I've become involved in writing, mostly poetry. www.kairostherapy.com.

Rebecca T. Dickinson "Grass from the Grave"
I've lived and worked in North and South Carolina. My dream and aspiration is to become an author. I've worked as a community news journalist. The loves of my life are my son and my fiancé. I continue to write and take care of my son, who saved my life.

Melissa Doffing "More to Lose"
Melissa Doffing is a stay at home mom and writer. She is co-editor of *Let Them Eat Crepes: stories featuring the French pancake.* She enjoys writing in all genres, but seems to do best in nonfiction. Recent publication credits include, *Salome Magazine, Savvy Women's Magazine,* and *A View from the Loft.* At the time of this bio, she's 16 weeks pregnant, keeping both fingers and legs crossed.

donnarkevic "Fetal Demise"
donnarkevic: Weston, WV. MFA National University. Recent poetry appeared in *Convergence Review, Earth Speak,* and *New Verse News.* Recent short story publications include *Colere and the Anthology, Seeking the Swan.* In 2005, Main Street Rag published, *Laundry,* a poetry chapbook. Also in 2005, *The Interview,* a play, won second place in the Playwright's Circle Competition.

Terri Elders "Dreaming as the Summer Dies"
Terri Elders, LCSW, lives in the country near Colville, WA with two dogs and three cats. In her MSW graduate work at UCLA in '77-'78 she interned at Los Angeles County Department of Adoptions. This triggered an ongoing interest in adult adoptees and the sealed record controversy. Terri's stories have appeared in dozens of anthologies, including multiple editions of the *Chicken Soup for the Soul, a Cup of Comfort* and the *Patchwork Path* series. She serves as a public member of the Washington State Medical Quality Assurance Commission. In 2006 she received the UCLA Alumni Association Community Service Award for her work with the Peace Corps. She blogs at http://atouchoftarragon.blogspot.com/.

Gail Rudd Entrekin "At Dawn he takes my Hand"
Gail Rudd Entrekin has an M.A. in English Literature from Ohio State University and has taught poetry and English literature at California

colleges for 25 years. Her collections of poems are *Change (Will Do You Good)* (Poetic Matrix Press, 2005), which was nominated for a Northern California Book Award, *You Notice the Body* (Hip Pocket Press, 1998), and *John Danced* (Berkeley Poets Workshop & Press, 1983). Poetry editor of Hip Pocket Press since 2000, she edits the press' online environmental literary magazine, *Canary* (www. hippocketpress.com/canary.cfm). She is the editor of the poetry & short fiction anthology *Sierra Songs & Descants: Poetry & Prose of the Sierra* (2002) and the poetry anthology *Yuba Flows* (2007). Her poems have been widely published in anthologies and literary magazines, including *Cimarron Review*, the *Ohio Journal* and *Southern Poetry Review*, and she and her husband, writer Charles Entrekin, live in the hills of San Francisco's East Bay.

Karen Ethelsdattar "The Single Mother and the Long Nightgown"
Karen Ethelsdattar is the author of three full length volumes of poetry, *Earthwalking & Other Poems, Thou Art a Woman & Other Poems,* and *Steam Rising Up from the Soul,* as well as three chapbooks, *The Cat Poems, Woman Artists and Woman as Art,* and *Poems of Peace & Protest.* Her individual poems have also appeared in a number of other publications. She is a New York and New Jersey based poet, writer, ritual maker and explorer of world spiritual traditions. She has a daughter & son, & grandson & granddaughter. She lives with her tortoise shell cat Cherie.

Kathy "ABBY"
I am a licensed psychotherapist and a community theater actor. I have two grown children and four grandsons. My daughter and her husband, the couple in the story, are doing very well. The addition of their second boy has not only seemed to heal some of the loss but add a joy they might never have known.

Kristine "Blood Loss"
I hope this can help women of all ages, especially teens, with the loss of a child. My pain never goes away, but knowing I can maybe ease someone else's pain helps. I would like to seriously thank Professor Jessica Williams for the confidence and courage to write about Domenick, she really helped me through.

Jamee Larson "Just Like Me"
Although it took me a long time and some very hard work to recover from my loss, I have now found a way to move on. I will never forget Jasmine, but I no longer allow that pain to consume me. I am currently completing my first year of graduate school at Minnesota State University Moorhead, studying creative writing. I am on track to graduate in 2013. Life can go on!

Daniel Lassell "Miss Carriage"
Daniel Lassell is a 22 year old, who recently graduated from Marian University with a Bachelor of Arts in English, now attending Marshall University to pursue a Master of Arts in English. He grew up in Eminence, Kentucky raising llamas and alpacas. Apart from school publications, he is also featured in *A Celebration of Young Poets* (Fall 2004), *riverrun Magazine* (May 2011) and *Pure Francis* (June 2011).

Lisa "Lovingly Placed" and "Forever, My Laura."
Lisa is the proud mom of two wonderful boys who came into her life through the miracle of adoption. When her children were small, Lisa returned to school and became a registered nurse. She is currently completing her graduate degree in community health. Lisa works with the pediatric special needs population.

Ed McManis "The Miscarriage"
I've worked with kids all my life; counselor, teacher, currently head of school at Sterne School, a school for students who learn differently. This poem is about my wife's miscarriage. We were shocked and stunned — never expected it. Our youngest son soon followed — complete joy, now in college. I often wonder about the child we didn't get to know.

Ryane Nicole "The Broken Crystal Ball and the Zombie Killer"
Ryane Nicole earned her MFA in creative writing from Antioch University, Los Angeles. She received her BA in English from Loyola Marymount University, where she also earned the Nikki Giovanni writing award and the honorable distinction of Valedictorian for the graduating class of 2000. Presently she teaches English at Golden West College and she is the proud mom of an active three-year-old son. Most importantly, she has learned that life's greatest lessons can indeed be taught by a child.

Catherine O'Neill "It's a Process"
I am at the point in my process where I am feeling more of a 'whatever happens, happens' mentality. It was a long process to get to, but I'm here...and I feel a million times better about it all.

Carl Palmer "Catachresis"
Carl Palmer, President of The Tacoma Writers Club, nominee for The Micro Award (Flash Fiction) and Three Pushcart Prizes (poetry) from Old Mill Road in Ridgeway Virginia, now lives in University Place Washington without wristwatch, cell phone or alarm clock — Carl's motto: long weekends forever.

Helen Peppe "The Starting Line"
Helen Peppe is a professional writer and photographer. She lives in Westbrook, Maine, with her two children, husband (yes The Eric of Starting Line) and her three dogs.

Deanna Perchyshyn "Gorgonzola"
Deanna Perchyshyn is a mom, wife, teacher, and writer in St.Paul Minnesota. Things have dramatically improved since her unplanned, college pregnancy. Now her oldest daughter is graduating college. It's been a rough but rewarding road.

Robyn Renee Riley "Adieu, Mon Petit Souvenir"
Robyn lives in Oklahoma with her husband and three children. Since her miscarriage she continues to contemplate her fertility.

Marit Rogne "To My Unborn"
Marit Rogne is a graduate of the school of the Art Institute of Chicago with a BFA in creative writing. She is currently an assistant editor at Gale/Cengage Learning. She has most recently published poetry with *Young American Poets* and *Red River Review*, and maintains a poetry blog a Maritsfuckingblogging.blogspot.com. She lives with her devilishly handsome boyfriend, fantastic best friend, and her four darling finches in Michigan. She enjoys dining establishments without television.

Rose "She's so Beautiful"
I'm still struggling with a sense of loss and guilt, but better. I was very young and in an abusive marriage. I didn't want to bring another child into my nightmare. I didn't know my true strengths like I do now. It

takes constant effort to keep looking forward towards the future, having learned one of life's biggest lessons.

Jason Sturner "Below Zero"
Jason Sturner was born and raised in the western suburbs of Chicago. In addition to poetry he writes short stories, music lyrics, and nature essays. He currently lives in Knoxville, Tennessee. Website: www.jasonsturner.blogspot.com.

Krista Wagner "My Baby"
I have 3 wonderful children. I am currently an English Professor married to a wonderful husband.

Aida Zilelian "In My Innocence"
I am a New York City writer, and started writing non-fiction, but eventually began writing short stories. Since my miscarriage, I have continued writing and have published short stories that can be found at www.aidazilelian.com.

Behind the Project

Melissa Ferina is a full time waitress, full time student, and a full time mother. She was inspired to start the Help Inspire Others project as she faced the challenge of single parenthood. The moment she found out she was pregnant at the age of 20, she became a single mother. Two years after her daughter was born, in 2007, she started the Help Inspire Others project as a means of telling her story and to learn about what others have been through. She saw this project as a full circle project. It not only gives support to those readers who are going through similar experiences but it is an outlet for those who submit. Many people who have submitted their story have felt a release within themselves. The project has become a positive conduit for many — and has already given support to those who need it. She continues to maintain the Help Inspire Others website (www.helpinspireothers.com) and receive stories for the next installment of her series. She hopes that people who read *paniK* are touched, inspired, and see a new perspective. She is on track to graduate in November 2011, with a certificate in cardiovascular ultrasound. She currently lives on Long Island with her husband and six-year-old daughter.